A Struggle Worthy
of Note

Recent Titles in
Contributions in Afro-American and African Studies

The Poet's Africa: Africanness in the Poetry of Nicolás Guillén and Aimé Césaire
Josaphat B. Kubayanda

Tradition and Modernity in the African Short Story: An Introduction to a Literature in Search of Critics
F. Odun Balogun

Politics in the African-American Novel: James Weldon Johnson, W.E.B. DuBois, Richard Wright, and Ralph Ellison
Richard Kostelanetz

Disfigured Images: The Historical Assault on Afro-American Women
Patricia Morton

Black Journalists in Paradox: Historical Perspectives and Current Dilemmas
Clint C. Wilson II

Dream and Reality: The Modern Black Struggle for Freedom and Equality
Jeannine Swift, editor

An Unillustrious Alliance: The African American and Jewish American Communities
William M. Phillips, Jr.

From Exclusion to Inclusion: The Long Struggle for African American Political Power
Ralph C. Gomes and Linda Faye Williams, editors

Mental and Social Disorder in Sub-Saharan Africa: The Case of Sierra Leone, 1787–1900
Leland V. Bell

The Racial Problem in the Works of Richard Wright and James Baldwin
Jean-François Gounard; Joseph J. Rodgers, Jr., translator

Renaissance Man from Louisiana: A Biography of Arna Wendell Bontemps
Kirkland C. Jones

A STRUGGLE WORTHY OF NOTE

The Engineering and Technological Education of Black Americans

DAVID E. WHARTON

Contributions in Afro-American and African Studies, Number 155

GREENWOOD PRESS
Westport, Connecticut • London

Library of Congress Cataloging-in-Publication Data

Wharton, David E.
    A struggle worthy of note : the engineering and technological
education of Black Americans / David E. Wharton.
       p. cm. — (Contributions in Afro-American and African
studies, ISSN 0069-9624 ; no. 155)
    Includes bibliographical references and index.
    ISBN 0-313-28207-2
    1. Afro-American engineers. 2. Afro-Americans—Education
(Higher)—United States. 3. Technical education—United States.
I. Title. II. Series.
TA157.W448   1992
620′.0089′96073—dc20   92-12524

British Library Cataloguing in Publication Data is available.

Library of Congress Catalog Card Number: 92-12524
ISBN: 0-313-28207-2
ISSN: 0069-9624

First published in 1992

Greenwood Press, 88 Post Road West, Westport, CT 06881
An imprint of Greenwood Publishing Group, Inc.

Printed in the United States of America

The paper used in this book complies with the
Permanent Paper Standard issued by the National
Information Standards Organization (Z39.48–1984).

10 9 8 7 6 5 4 3 2 1

Contents

Illustrations

EXHIBITS

TABLES

Preface

I recently attended a conference on blacks in engineering at a well-known Boston school of engineering. The well-intentioned speeches were followed by a short address by the dean of the college. He chose to cover the same timeworn topics that I have heard from nearly every dean of every formerly all-white school of engineering. First they speak of the scant numbers of blacks in the field of engineering and then go on to tell of the valiant strides their school now takes to insure that blacks, hispanics, and other minorities are included in the student mix.

By the end of the address you are completely confused. You wonder why more blacks are not clamoring for inclusion or why there are not more older black engineers who could point the way for the new generation. The likelihood that most of the participants in that conference understood the legacy of America's century-long, two-tiered educational system seemed slight. Nor did there seem to be a high level of appreciation for the fact that one of the major causes for the meager representation of blacks in engineering lies with the institution, not the individual. The conference room in which we sat is part of an institution that until recently had treated black applicants as pariahs.

American higher education, the fount to which all prospective engineers in this country must come, has been a preserve of the white power structure since its inception. It was made so by whites, not by blacks. It was made so by the exclusion of blacks from the preparatory programs that lead to full participation in the fields of technology. For many years, the long struggle to overturn this system was continuously opposed by those in positions of power in the educational community. That struggle continues today.

Far from a new struggle, the denial of opportunity preceded the campus and is rooted in the patterns of slavery. To deny another human being literacy is an inhumane act, yet it was the law that made millions of enslaved blacks intellectual prisoners during and after their tenure as American slaves. For years after the Emancipation, blacks would still be forced to depend on whites for their educational sustenance. Few inroads would be made during the first seventy-five years of freedom.

By 1870, over 1200 colleges had come into existence in the United States. There is little evidence that any black ever attended any of these institutions (Weinberg, 1979, p. 263). With few notable exceptions, this pattern of exclusion of blacks from higher education continued well into the twentieth century. For those who wished to enter the fields of technology, the record is worse. Racial exclusion was not a practice generated and practiced exclusively by former southern slaveholders. Rather, this was a widespread practice known to exist in the most prestigious schools. As late as 1940, with a single exception, black faculty were to be found only on black college campuses. As late as 1946 at the University of Chicago, the respected sociologist William F. Ogburn made the assertion that all white graduate students would withdraw if a black was appointed to the faculty (Weinberg, 1979, p. 288).

As late as 1970 many of the authors of the texts on which American educational philosophy was built were products of a system born of division and exclusion. Many knew little or nothing of the darker tenth of the nation, yet they wrote inclusively of American academia.

At least two examples of the resulting oversight of black contributions rest at the doors of Lawrence R. Veysey and Frederick Rudolph. Both are authors of works chronicling the higher education history of our nation. Rudolph's 1962 work *The American College and University: A History* and Veysey's 1965 *The Emergence of The American University* for many years were cornerstones of educational readings. When Rudolph refers to Harvard University in his 516-page compendium, he does so with more than seventy entries; for Yale, more than sixty; and for the University of Chicago, more than twenty-five. When Rudolph speaks of black colleges he cites only Howard and Fisk Universities, includes them on one page, and does not speak of them again. There is no mention of Atlanta University, Morehouse College, or any other black school. It is as if they did not exist. Veysey, an author whose work traced American higher education until the early decades of this century, makes no mention of either Howard or Fisk though both were viable institutions as early as 1910. Nor does he mention any other school that might cause his readers to believe that there was a black constituency abroad in the land. These omissions of relevant materials concerning black efforts for educational fulfillment in many of the standard texts became an accepted and damaging method of portraying black people.

This meant that at the highest levels of academia the omission of black people from the espoused history was endorsed and approved. As the director of a minority engineering program I searched for two years to find a text that would enhance the self-esteem of incoming freshmen, a text that would tell of the history of contributions of American blacks to the field of engineering—no such book existed. It is time that a new history was written. This is a beginning effort to examine one small area of higher education: engineering and technological education.

It is important to tell the stories of black inventors and of the evolution of engineering and technological education for blacks. These stories, like so many other stories of American blacks, must be exhumed, written, and located in the larger story, the story of America. Without them, our history is weaker, or worse, a lie. Without them, a significant number of our people have no sense of hope or control over their own destinies.

After all, this is a record of people coming to grips with society's inadequacies and inequities and moving beyond these to a participatory role in the nation's technological and engineering community. This recounting can also serve to increase the understanding and the critical appreciation of a system that had the power to withhold membership or ignore worthy contributions of certain individuals while advancing and promoting other participants in the world of technology.

I view this work as an important task because far too often black students, as well as the black community at large, are introduced to a world in which the vast majority of heroes are white. Black students deserve more; they need to know that black expertise has played a role in America's growth. They need to hear of the victory over educational tyranny that is part of their legacy. But most of all, this work is important to me because without it I, too, become part of those who withhold the truth from the young.

Today, the legal barriers to segregated education have been torn away, and institutional behavior comes under greater scrutiny. In spite of this, I am under no illusions that present-day students do not suffer many of the same indignities as their predecessors.

Chapter 1

Inventors and Tinkers

The Emancipation Proclamation initiated a new era for Americans, an era in which all men could not only receive the blessings of liberty but also make meaningful contributions to those institutions that were the guarantors of that liberty. For former slaves, both propositions held a measure of unreality. To be regarded as the political equal of former slave owners was something to be hoped for, not realized. To be able to contribute to the framework that supported such parity was, for many, beyond comprehension. The blessings that were forthcoming were sparse—often negligible. Every concession by former masters would have to be won through struggle, but this was to be expected in the new era.

The right to contribute to this new institution of freedom should have been available to all, but in many cases the gifts of the emancipated were unwanted. Those talents and gifts that had sustained and improved a way of life for much of America for two centuries—talents and gifts that had been prized during the many years of black servitude—were now to be squandered because provisions for their productive use in the free market had never been planned. Talents and gifts that displayed brains more than brawn, tenacity more than tempo, were spurned. The idea that a former slave could make a significant contribution to his new nation has taken more than a century to find root in the American psyche.

Exhibit 1
**A Letter from the U.S. Attorney General to the Commissioner of Patents,
June 10, 1858**

                                        C O P Y
                                        K. W.

                    INVENTION OF A SLAVE

A new and useful machine invented by a slave cannot be
                      patented

                    Attorney General's Office
                         June 10, 1858

Sir:
        I fully concur with the Commissioner of Patents in the
opinion he has given on the application of Mr. O.T.E.
Stewart of Mississippi. For the reasons given by the
Commissioner, I think as he does, that a machine invented by
a slave, though it be new and useful, cannot, in the present
state of the law, be patented. I may add that if such a
patent was issued to the master, it would not protect him in
the courts against persons who might infringe it.
                                Very respectfully yours,
                                        J.S. Black
Hon. Jacob Thompson,
        Secretary of the Interior

   During the time of slavery the inventiveness of slaves, although
encouraged by slaveholders, was never fully documented. The law
did not permit slaves to receive any recognition for their contributions. The protection of patent rights did not extend to slaves. A
letter from the U.S. Attorney General's office to the Commissioner
of Patents dated June 10, 1858, makes this point quite clear
(Exhibit 1). Another letter, postmarked September 16, 1903, from
Isaiah Montgomery to Henry Baker, also of the Patent Office,
shows that the inventions of slaves were put to use and at times
became commercial successes (Exhibit 2).

   The battle for parity continues to this day. Looking at America's
training of our industrial and technical forces, one can discern the
high price that this denial of opportunity has exacted and passed
onto succeeding generations. One can also see the systematic
destruction of hope for technical education in those communities
most affected by this denial.

Exhibit 2
**A letter from Isaiah Montgomery of Mound Bayou, Mississippi, to Henry
Baker, U.S. Patent Office, September 16, 1903**

```
            DEPARTMENT  OF  THE  INTERIOR
            UNITED STATES LAND OFFICE
                Jackson, Miss., Sept. 16, 1903
```

Mr. Henry K Baker
Room 236, Patent Office,
        Washington City

My dear sir-
            Through the courtesy of my friend, Mr. R.D.
Littlejohn of Columbus, I am in receipt of your interesting
letter of the 9th last. And I would say in reply, that my
father, Benjamin T. Montgomery, had several articles before
the U.S. Patent office; those presented previous to the war
were looked after by Mr. Jefferson Davis (of Confederate
States ----), he experienced considerable trouble in
presenting articles for a Patent a slave, which I have
always thought was responsible for that clause of the
Confederate States Constitution, which allowed patents to be
issued in the name of slaves.
            The articles to which you refer consisted of a system
of walking paddles for the propulsion of boats; the patent
was not pressed after the war owing to the opinion of many
boatmen that the paddles could not be sufficiently protected
from damage by drift, and other and other floating
substances; but my father constructed two boats(handled by
man power) using double pulls, and operating the paddles
between them, which proved quite superior to the propelling
power of cars. Mr. Davis designated the swiftest of these
boats the Nautilus, owing to its likeness to that fish or
water creature. You may also cross some improvements in the
cotton bale ----- which were handled by Munn and Co., after
the war.
            Another Montgomery, Peter T., brother of my father, had
a ditching plow------------- in the 6th Auditor's office)
has secured a device for holding books, papers, etc., to be
read or copied with a typewriter. If you could run across
him up there, he will be able to talk interestingly about
all of the cases above referred to.
            I shall be quite glad to have a few copies of the issue
of the Post containing your article, and will pay the cost
of the same if sent to my home address, Mound Bayou, Miss..
(Bolivar County)
                        Very respectfully yours,
                        Isaiah Montgomery

An examination of history will show that American minorities
have made significant contributions to the industrial growth of this
country despite the restrictions imposed by society.

Contributions made in engineering by minorities are numerous
and have occurred in many of the industries where blacks have

participated. Prior to the recent increase in minority engineers, many of the contributors were not college graduates. The early contributors were called "tinkers." The term does not fully describe the intricacies of their work.

During the late nineteenth and early twentieth centuries tinkers accounted for the creation of many of the labor-saving devices that aided in the growth of American industry. Today, they would be considered research and development engineers. Among the contributors were:

- Andrew Baird, inventor of the Jenny coupler, an automatic device which secures two train cars when they are bumped.

- Frederick McKinley Jones, inventor of the first mechanical refrigeration units for railroad cars and trucks.

- Garrett A. Morgan, inventor of the gas mask.

- Grantville Woods, inventor of the incubator, which revolutionized the egg industry, and the Synchronous Multiplex Telegraph, a device designed to avert railway collisions.

- Jan Matzeliger, inventor of the shoe-lasting machine, a machine that revolutionized the industry.

- H. C. Webb, inventor of the grubber, a labor-saving piece of farm machinery that had great application in the early twentieth century. (Harris, 1974, p. 114)

Certainly the contributions of these six do not begin to show the breadth of involvement of American minorities in engineering in the years following the Civil War. To demonstrate that, it would be necessary to begin with eggbeaters (W. Johnson, Patent #292821) and include such items as the automatic gearshift (R. D. Spikes, Patent #1,889,814), the self-binding harvesting machine (William Douglass, Patent #789,010), or the steam gauge (O'Conner and Turner, Patent #566,615) (Harris, 1974, pp. 110–12).

In the South, prior to the Civil War, most of the industrial labor, both agricultural and mechanical, was performed by slaves. Consequently, most of the artisans, mechanics, skilled, and ordinary laborers were black. From this group came a variety of mechanical labor-saving devices. Though it may be groundless, there has always been the persistent rumor that the cotton gin was Eli Whitney's in name only.

For nearly fifty years after the Civil War, blacks made significant but unpublicized contributions to the industrial retooling of America. In as many cases as not, blacks refused to accept the notoriety that came with their contributions for fear of rejection by the commercial market. By so doing, the needs and contributions of many are a part of history that has been lost.

One outstanding inventor whose work would not be hidden was Grantville Woods, the inventor of the telegraph, and holder, during his lifetime, of over fifty patents. His notoriety came as much from his inventions as the court cases they caused.

GRANTVILLE WOODS (1856–1910)

Grantville Woods was born in Columbus, Ohio, on April 23, 1856. By the age of 10 he had begun his working life as a machine-shop employee spending his evenings attending school or receiving private instruction (Logan, 1982, p. 663). At 16 he went to Missouri and worked as a fireman and engineer. He also worked in New York City as a machine-shop employee and in a Springfield, Illinois, steel mill. During all of this time he continued to pursue electrical and mechanical engineering courses. Shortly before his twenty-second birthday, Woods embarked on a long tour aboard the steamship *Ironsides*, returning in 1884, at which time he and his brother Lyates opened their own machine shop in Cincinnati. It was now time for the engineering lessons to pay dividends.

Woods was to become the most celebrated inventor of his day, but throughout his life there would be those who would deny both his inventiveness and his race. In April 1895, *Cosmopolitan* magazine claimed he was "notable for his ancestry" (pp. 761–62). The article claimed his mother's father was Malay Indian and "his other grandparents were by birth, full blooded savages, Australian aborigines born in the wilds back of Melbourne" (Balch, 1895, p. 762)—this in order to claim he had little or no African-American ancestry (Christopher, 1895, p. 270). Interestingly, the *Cosmopolitan* article claims that Woods, as a boy of 10, began his career operating the bellows at an Australian railroad repair yard. It goes on to tell of his family's emigration to America when he was 16, making the year of his family's migration 1872. The likelihood of a black Aborigine/Malay Indian family migrating from Australia to America and deciding to settle in Missouri, a former slave state, seems extremely slight.

Industrialists realized long before this *Cosmopolitan* article that Woods' inventions had wide application in American industry (Christopher, 1981, p. 270). But to advance a black American inventor in the era following the Civil War would have been difficult. *Cosmopolitan*'s reconstructed youth and family history was one way of avoiding the confrontation, but Woods, in a biographical sketch in Simmons' *Men of Mark*, published in 1887, set the record straight (Logan, 1982, p. 665). Woods was a native of Columbus, Ohio, where he apprenticed as a machinist and a blacksmith. There is nothing in this account of Woods' life to suggest Australian ancestry.

After succeeding at progressively demanding jobs and classes in electronics, mechanical, and electrical engineering, Woods became a locomotive engineer on the Danville & Southern Railroad. In 1884 he received his first patent for a steam boiler furnace. His next two patents were awarded for an incubator capable of hatching 50,000 eggs at once, and a telephone transmitter much like the ones in use today. He experimented with circuit design and the generation of electricity. Two results of this work were the Automatic Safety Cut-Outs for electrical circuits and a "System of Electrical Distribution." In April 1888 he received a patent for a galvanic battery.

He contributed to the development of the "third rail"; he invented an automatic air brake for railway systems; and in 1892 he introduced a complete electric railway that operated at Coney

Island. The railway had no exposed wires, secondary batteries, or slotted way.

His most important invention was the Synchronous Multiplex Railway Telegraph. This invention became the radar system for the railroads, notifying trains and station masters of the relative positions of their rolling stock. He was hailed as a genius and, in his time, given greater acclaim than Bell, Westinghouse, or Edison. But his success was to be short-lived (Christopher, 1981, p. 270).

Woods founded the Woods' Electric Company after successfully fending off the challenge of Thomas Alva Edison, who claimed the right to the telegraph. Woods' invention was a telephone transmitter that produced a more distinct sound and greater effects than the Bell instrument. With Woods' instrument it was possible to speak over the same wires used for Morse code transmission. Yet Woods found it difficult to maintain an enterprise during the late nineteenth and early twentieth century (Christopher, 1981, p. 269–76). In a national climate in which lynchings and segregation were rampant, any minority who competed with whites was deemed a threat to the status quo and someone to be dealt with. And so it was with Woods. In the end he would succumb to the economic tyranny that large, influential bankers would apply. But in 1895, if never again, Woods had a victorious day in court.

Among the many inventions that he marketed was a dynamotor, a revolutionary apparatus for the time. As *Cosmopolitan* reported it,

> Certain features of this invention are now involved in interference proceedings in the United States Patent Office with five rival inventors. Of these, only one had the invention perfected to the extent of using the dynamotor. This one is Dr. Schuyler S. Wheeler of the Crocker-Wheeler Electric Company. The proceedings, however, showed that Woods completely developed his invention when there was no prior model to guide him, and when the others were, at most, only taking the preliminary steps which led them years later in the same direction. The Crocker-Wheeler Company was forced

to accept Mr. Woods as a partner in order to retain the improvements independently invented by Dr. Wheeler. (Balch, 1895, p. 762)

On this occasion in 1895 Woods prevailed but his fortunes would change dramatically. Woods could not raise money to finance the business that his inventions might have fostered. As a result, he was forced to sell his patent for the electric railway to Thomas Edison's General Electric Company; his telephone to the American Bell Telephone Company; and his electric brakes to Westinghouse Electric Company (Christopher, 1981, p. 275). Once the sale of the patent rights was completed no vestige of the black inventor was left, and, as a result, generations of Americans, both black and white, have had little or no knowledge of the contributions of this inventor.

To have been deprived of the notoriety that comes with the uniqueness of the inventions was not new to blacks. Since the institution of slavery the practice had always been to distance blacks from any of the residuals of their contributions. In this case, however, slavery had been abolished, but in the eyes of the industrialists Woods' name would not enhance the acceptance of the product. Instead, the electric railway bore the name of Edison, the telephone bore the name of Bell, and to this day many believe that the Westinghouse electric brake is an invention of that firm. Not only was Woods denied the deserved praise for his work, others presented his inventions as products of their labor.

As an example of Woods' ability, consider the following inventions and the industrial entities to which they were assigned:

Electric Railway System to American Engineering Co., 1891

Electric Railway Conduit to Universal Electric Co., 1883

System of Electrical Distribution to S. E. Riley, 1896

Electric Railway to General Electric, 1901, 1902, 1904

Electric Railway System to Electro Magnetic Traction Co., 1901

Regulating and Controlling Electrical Translating Devices to Harry Ward Leonard, 1901, 1902

System of Electrical Control to Townsend-Decker Trustees, 1904
Patents for Railway Brake Apparatus to Westinghouse, 1904, 1905
Two Patents for Safety Apparatus to General Electric, 1906
Vehicle Controlling Device to General Electric, 1907

Woods stands as the black inventor responsible for the most patents applied for and granted and he is noted for the wide and varied areas of interest he pursued. But Woods is not the only black inventor of the time who made significant contributions. At least four additional contributors can be included with him: Lewis H. Latimer, Garrett A. Morgan, Jan Matzeliger, and H. C. Webb.

LEWIS LATIMER (1848–1928)

Lewis Latimer was born in Chelsea, Massachusetts, on September 4, 1848, the son of a slave who had escaped from Virginia and gone to Boston. Lewis and his mother were abandoned in 1858, when he was 10 years old. He was able to get an education by enrolling in a farm school. Later he joined the Navy and saw action on the James River aboard the U.S.S. *Massasoit*. Honorably discharged in 1865, he found, after many disappointments, a job as office boy in the firm of Brosby and Gould, patent solicitors. Purchasing a set of secondhand drafting tools and reading available books, Latimer asked his employers to permit him to do some drawings. The request was granted and he was given a desk with an increase in pay. The office where he was employed was located near the school where Alexander Graham Bell was conducting experiments on the telephone. They become friends and, according to contemporaries of Latimer, Bell asked him to draw each part of the telephone that Bell was perfecting to illustrate how it worked. When the drawing and the machine were completed, Bell was granted a patent in 1876.

In 1880 Latimer was employed by the United States Electric Lighting Company, Bridgeport, Connecticut, where he worked with Hiram S. Maxim. Latimer invented carbon filaments for the

Maxim electric incandescent lamp and obtained a patent for them in 1881; he also invented a cheap method for making the filaments. Maxim and an associate raised money to set up factories to manufacture Latimer's inventions, which were used in railroad stations in the United States, Canada, and other countries.

Latimer began his association with Thomas Alva Edison in 1883, serving as an engineer, chief draftsman, and expert witness on the Board of Patent Control in gathering evidence against the infringement of patents held by Westinghouse and General Electric. Latimer was one of the first to be selected for the formation of the Edison Pioneers, a hand-picked group of investigators assigned to difficult technical tasks; he was the only black member. A "Statement of the Edison Pioneers" on the occasion of his death, December 11, 1928, ended:

> Broad-mindedness, versatility in the accomplishment of things intellectual and cultural, a linguist, a devoted husband and father, all were characteristics of him, and his genial presence will be missed from our gatherings (Logan, 1982, p. 386).

GARRETT MORGAN (1875–1963)

Garrett Morgan was born and raised on a farm in Paris, Kentucky. At the age of 14 Morgan, with only six weeks of schooling, went to Cincinnati where he worked as a handyman for a wealthy landowner. The job allowed him to hire a tutor to help him with his grammar. In 1895 he moved to Cleveland where in 1908 he married Mary Anne Hassek, who lived with him at 5202 Harlem Avenue Northwest for most of the next fifty-five years. It was here that he patented his inventions.

His first job in Cleveland, as a sewing machine adjuster for a clothing manufacturer, sparked his lifelong interest and skill with things mechanical. Morgan lived a quiet life in Cleveland, devoting himself to his family and his love of tinkering. The first of his many inventions was introduced to the public on July 25, 1916. On that day, an explosion ripped through a Cleveland waterworks tunnel 250 feet below Lake Erie, trapping several workmen. Two

rescue attempts were made by the city's police and fire departments. Nine of the eleven would-be rescuers were killed by ex-
ploding gases. After the second attempt failed, Morgan was called
to the disaster and was asked to use his 1914 invention, the Morgan
Safety Hood. He was able to save three workmen trapped in the
gas- and smoke-filled tunnels. They were carried to safety by
Morgan and rescuers wearing the safety hood (Logan, 1982, p.
453).

Morgan first appeared with his safety hood and smoke protector,
the forerunner of the gas mask, in 1912, and improved his invention over the next two years. The safety hood, designed for speedy
work, had no valves to adjust, no bindings about the neck, no straps
to buckle, and no heavy tanks of air. It could be put on or taken off
as easily as tipping your hat. The hood could be donned in seven
seconds and taken off in three. The protective hood had an air
supply that allowed a rescuer to stand in the midst of suffocating
gases for fifteen to twenty minutes, and could be adapted for use
when spraying deadly chemicals. Morgan's "Breathing Device"
was granted a patent in 1914 (Logan, 1982, p. 453).

After the 1916 lifesaving performance of his perfected mask,
Morgan's National Safety Device Company produced it and fire
departments, both here and abroad, purchased and used his invention. He traveled from state to state demonstrating his gas mask.
However, racial attitudes in many southern states forced him to
hire a white man to demonstrate his invention, while he passed for
an Indian. When it became widely known that the gas mask's
inventor was black, Morgan's production was severely slowed. In
the South, sales virtually ended. The gas mask found new life when
the government used the invention in World War I to protect
soldiers from deadly chlorine gas fumes. Ironically, the wartime
use of the invention more than compensated for the civilian
boycott.

Morgan later received a patent for his three-way automatic
traffic signal. It was a totally new idea that went beyond the usual
"stop-go" designations. His signal incorporated, for the first time,
a "caution," or yellow light, and it required no one to attend it. In

addition to his American patent, patents were granted in Canada and England. He sold his rights to the signal in 1923 to General Electric for $40,000 (Logan, 1982, p. 452).

For his work as an inventor Morgan received the First Grand Prize Gold Medal from the National Safety Device Company at the Second International Exposition of Safety and Sanitation in 1914, honorary membership in the International Association of Fire Engineers, a United States government citation for his traffic signal, and national recognition at the Emancipation Centennial Celebration in Chicago in September 1963 (Logan, 1982, p. 453).

JAN MATZELIGER (1852–1889)

Jan Matzeliger emigrated to the United States from Dutch Guiana in the 1870s, and worked as a shoemaker's apprentice in Philadelphia and New York. When he was 25 he moved to Lynn, Massachusetts, to work in the shoe industry. After five years as a factory worker and part-time tinker, he invented a machine that was to revitalize the American shoe industry. Prior to the invention of his shoe-lasting machine, the shoe industry relied totally on hand lasting to join the shoe uppers to the sole. This meant that the skill was kept in the hands of a few artisans and that the competition among shoe manufacturers for reasonable pricing was limited. Matzeliger's machine was the initial step toward the automation of the industry and far surpassed any previous effort to upgrade and streamline the process. His machine would cut, sew, and tack shoes, arrange the heels, drive the nails, and deliver the finished product, all in a minute's time. The invention meant a 50 percent reduction in the price of shoes, a doubling of the wages of shoe workers, and an improvement in the working conditions for an entire industry. He was offered, but refused, $1,500 for his original invention. In 1883 Matzeliger patented his lasting machine (Baker, 1969, p. 226).

Matzeliger realized the far-reaching effects of his new invention and began to set up a stock corporation to market the machine. He never realized the deserved wealth from his enterprise because of his lack of business experience and his poor health leading to an early death. Businessmen were quick to purchase all of the stock of his company, laying the foundation for the organization of the United Shoe Machinery Company (USM), the largest and most productive company of its kind in the world (Baker, 1906, pp. 10–12).

The invention was bought by the USM and little was ever said of the inventor once USM acquired the patent. In October 1889 the *Lynn News* (Mass.) reported that the United Shoe Machine Company had erected a school specifically designed to instruct students in this new technology. Classes of 200 were common. Upon graduation the students were dispatched to various parts of the world to instruct others in the workings of this new Matzeliger Shoe-Lasting Machine. The machine was a marvel of complexity and belied the lack of formal engineering education of its inventor. Jan Matzeliger had gained his appreciation for machinery by working in machine shops throughout New England (*Crisis*, August 1913, p. 7). He died a young man of 36, leaving much of his stock to the North Congregational Society of Lynn, Massachusetts. Due to the magnitude of his invention, there were those who never admitted the Matzeliger was black. It required a certified copy of his death certificate to prove what many had known: the shoe industry had been revitalized by the invention of a black man.

H. C. WEBB

The last of these inventors was H. C. Webb, the inventor of the Webb Palmetto Grubbing Machine. This machine represented the newest in farming technology in 1916. American farming had always been a labor-intensive undertaking, and attempts to reduce its dependence on a now-free labor force were always welcomed. This was also a time when America began to see the possibility of being drawn into a war that would limit the availability of farm labor. Webb's invention drastically reduced the need for large numbers of farm hands for the preparation of the soil for crops. It also reduced the number of persons needed to tend the crops during the growing season.

Webb was not a college engineering graduate. He had obtained his experience as a worker in sawmills and blacksmith shops and his natural inclination toward farming implements gathered over sixteen years spent as a farm laborer in his native North Carolina (*Crisis*, February 1917, p. 10).

By listing these inventors it is obvious that black Americans did make significant technological contributions. Obvious, too, is the lack of recognition that these men received during and after their moments of greatness. These inventors show that an unharnessed supply of technical expertise always existed in the black community. Given the correct exposure, these black contributors could have served as role models for a generation of black youngsters. Their lack of recognition has meant that succeeding generations of black Americans have no knowledge of their technological past.

Fortunately, there were those who worked to bring these inventions to a wider, more appreciative audience. Chief among these were Henry E. Baker and C. H. Duell of the Department of the Interior.

HENRY E. BAKER, U.S. PATENT OFFICE: RECORDER OF BLACK PROGRESS

Henry Baker is an important figure in the development of black engineering in America. As a middle-management employee of the Department of the Interior, he corresponded with white professionals who under other circumstances might not have acknowledged him. Because of his dedication, Baker compiled evidence of hundreds of black patent holders, inventors, and technological contributors. Baker, through his correspondence, reveals the attitudes of several patent attorneys. This is important since they were the agents with whom inventors worked in order to have their inventions registered.

Baker's work between 1900 and 1910 came at a time when, across the city from his workplace, Howard University was introducing its

Exhibit 3
A letter from attorney E. J. O' Brien, St. Louis, Missouri, to C. H. Duell,
Commissioner of Patents, February 9, 1900

```
E.J. O'BRIEN                          Patent Law a Specialty
ATTORNEY AT LAW
304 N. EIGHTH STREET
ROOM 34 TURNER BUILDING
                                      ST. LOUIS, Feby 9, 1900
Hon C.H. Duell
        Commissioner
Dear Sir:
      In 30 yrs experience in patent practice I never met a
Negro inventor in St. Louis or elsewhere.
      Organically the Negro is like the Mongolian, he is an
imitator and not an originator.  I have known negroes who
were the most reliable of men to keep an engine i.e.(a steam
engine) up to its best capacity. But such were instructed,
and developed nothing beyond what was given them by others.
      May be that is because of location Missouri being on
the borderline twixt bondman and free in former times their
minds, while susceptible of the originating or inventive
faculty here could not find root because of the ----- of
caste, and its natural sequences. But I doubt it.It could be
demonstrated if so, farther north. So I don't know any negro
inventors, and I don't think I ever will.
                                     Yours truly,
                                     E.J. O'Brien
```

first courses in engineering. To initiate these courses, a grant from the federal government was required, and Baker's work was available as proof of black participation in technological fields.

In 1900, under the guidance of C. H. Duell, the then Commissioner of Patents, the Department of the Interior sought to locate black patent holders to exhibit their inventions in a "Negro Exhibit" at the Paris Exhibition. On June 26, 1900, letters were sent to patent attorneys in an effort to get some idea of the availability of black inventions and inventors. The replies to Duell's questionnaire reveal much about the racial climate at the turn of the century. There were those who said they had heard of or knew of one or two patent holders, but in the main, their letters were like that of attorney E. J. O'Brien of St. Louis, Missouri, who dismissed the question as absurd (Exhibit 3).

Much of what has been preserved about the early black inventors is due to the work of this man. Not much is known about Baker except that he was a cadet at the Naval Academy in 1875 but was forced to leave in 1877 as a result of the white prejudice that he found at the Academy. In 1877 he was hired as a copyist at the U.S. Patent Office. In 1879 he entered Harvard Law School, graduating in 1881. He returned to the Patent Office and rose to the position of Second Examiner (Baker, 1969, p. 1). In that position he was responsible for much of what is known about black inventors of his day (Baker, 1969, p. 11).

Baker aided black congressman George H. Murray in the compilation of material that allowed the congressman to enter into the *Congressional Record* on August 10, 1894, the particulars of more than ninety patents held by black inventors. By 1900 Baker had compiled a substantial resource of black inventors and planned to publish his findings on the fiftieth anniversary of the Emancipation Proclamation in 1915. In his quest for a more complete listing of contributors, and since there was no mention of race on the patent application, Baker decided to write to patent attorneys asking for help in locating persons he might have overlooked.

During the years 1911–1913 Baker corresponded with more than 8,000 of the 12,000 patent attorneys in America, and over 2,500 replied. Most of Baker's replies were similar to O'Brien's response sent to Duell ten years earlier. Most said that they had never heard of a colored inventor, and more than a few said that they never expected to hear from one (Baker, 1969, p. 11). Perhaps the most pointed reply came from patent attorney B. J. Nolan of 320 Temple Court, Chattanooga, Tennessee, on June 26, 1913 (Exhibit 4).

Mr. Nolan's remarks have been catalogued as part of a larger Carter G. Woodson Collection at the Library of Congress. Replies from other attorneys are also available. F. E. Stebbins, of Stebbins and Wright of Washington, D.C., replied that he knew of no black inventors but that he did recall the denial of a patent to a slave inventor (Exhibit 5). Replies from Frank R. Williams of Syracuse, New York, George Lamar of the District of Columbia, and Robert Hood of Cedarville, Ohio, were perhaps the most vile (Exhibits 6, 7, 8). Hood's stationery identifies him as a lawyer, consulting engineer, and surveyor. His remarks identify him as a racist.

Exhibit 4
A letter from B. J. Nolan, Chattanooga, Tennessee, to E. B. Moore,
Commissioner of Patents, June 26, 1913

```
B.J. Nolan
    320 Temple Court
      Chattanooga, Tenn.

6/26 1913
I never knew a Negro to even suggest a new idea.  Much less
to patent one.  And I have dealt with them all my life.

                                          B.J. Nolan
P.S. I have asked other lawyers around me for data on Negro
inventions.  And they took it as a joke.
                                          B.J.N.
```

Exhibit 5
A letter from attorney F. E. Stebbins of Stebbins and Wright,
Washington, D.C., to C.H. Duell, Commissioner of Patents

```
Stebbins & Wright
    Washington,
              D.C.

Honorable Commissioner of Patents
Sir: The first invention by a negro for which protection was
sought came before the Office in connection with an
application filed by the negro's master.  The master was
referred to the Attorney General and all dates can readily
be found by consulting the index to Attorney General's
Reports. Although no patent issued the fact may be of
interest in connection with information about colored
inventors.

                                   Respectfully,
                                     F.B. Stebbins
```

It is important to note that if any of the respondents used a fountain pen to reply, he was using the invention of W. B. Purvis, whose invention had been patented twenty-three years earlier (Harris, 1974, p. 110). If he wrote in pencil, he may have used a pencil sharpener, the brainchild of another black inventor, J. L. Love. Love's patent had been granted sixteen years before Mr. Nolan wrote his letter (Harris, 1974, p. 111).

Still, it was Nolan's attitude that prevailed. The racism of Nolan and his colleagues would soon expand to provide the barriers to minority access to the specialization and sophistication that indus-

Exhibit 6
A letter from engineer/attorney Robert Hood, Cedarville, Ohio, to the Commissioner of Patents, June 25, 1910

```
Law Office
R. Hood
Consulting Engineer
Surveyor

                              Cedarville, Ohio June 25, 1910

Honorable Commissioner of Patents,
     Answering your request for information I have to say,
No colored person within my knowledge is an inventor, and
none that I know of has ever made any effort in that
direction.
     My personal experience in Ohio with them for 18 years
is that their elevation to good citizenship is a failure.  I
have tried here in ----- Co. with others to form a colored
Y.M.C.A. at Cedarville where of a population of about 1400
we have about 400 niggers, we started with 17 after about 3
months effort we ended with 0. I then tried to form a bible
class of Outside Young Buck niggers that also was a failure.
The 15th Amendment has helped to make them hauty, lazy,
supercilious, lack of the elements of good citizenship.
Shows that with half a century of freedom, with few
exceptions, the draft remains licentious, criminal.
     In the widest sense the doctrine that human destiny
turns on the theory of personal responsibility is incumbent
on both white and black.  It seems that more than half a
century is required to awaken them to the great fact that
with full citizenship under the 15th Amendment they have
failed to discover this great so immediately at the basis of
destiny.
                              Faithfully,
                              Robt. Hood
```

trial America demanded. To the innocent onlooker, the strides that minority tinker/inventors were making were the natural progression for former mechanics who were thoroughly familiar with many of the implements that they improved or surpassed. To the more astute observer, there was a different interpretation.

For blacks who may have had leanings toward engineering or the technologies, an entire cadre of role models were passing from view. Though their contributions would continue to insure a better way of life for most Americans, any association with black inventors would be obliterated.

Most American schoolchildren would grow up learning of Bell and Edison and never hear the names of Woods, Latimer, or

Exhibit 7
A letter from attorney Frank R. Williams to E. B. Moore, Commissioner of Patents

```
Frank R. Williams
535 Clinton St.
Syracuse, N.Y.

I do not know of any colored men who have taken out patents,
although I know a number of colored men who have made
practical improvements, and some of which might have been
patented, which were used to practical and public benefit.
    I am one of few white men(grandson of ---- soldier and
son of a man who wanted abolition at first election
thereof,) who can personally say that " I have had colored
men working for me, I have worked for and under colored
men,(one case, a colored man foreman over 85 white men, in
machine manufacturing) and all I know of experience with
colored men and women -------. Let me hear more of this.
                                              Frank R. Williams
```

Exhibit 8
A letter from George H. Lamar, Washington, D.C., to E. B. Moore, Commissioner of Patents, 1913

```
Geo H. Lamar
Federal Building
Wash. City

    I am unable to supply any information on the subject.
I know of no accounts of the African race.
    As a son of a slaveholder of the south and a more or
less observer of the negro during my life of 45 years, I am
impressed with the idea that the negro is an apt imitator
but not ordinarily given to constructive or original lines
of thought.
    Some are good mechanics-------------.
                                              George H. Lamar
```

Matzeliger. As Bell and Edison served to inspire the inquisitive minds of some children, Woods, Latimer, and Matzeliger would have been equally powerful in shaping the futures of countless others. There are many points along this continuum where losses such as this may seem inconsequential. They are not. The lingering effects of the lack of recognition, the inability to secure financing, the elimination of the true identity of many contributors, and the phase-out of many black role models meant that blacks could not look with the pride of ownership at the new technologies. The lesson to be learned from these occurrences was that in the world of technology blacks were consumers, not contributors.

Many of these inventions came during the first two decades of this century, a time when black education was being influenced by many groups. If technological contributions were to continue from the black community, a new educational system would be needed. Philanthropists, missionaries, black leaders, and church groups all demanded a voice in the structuring of the educational format of black Americans. Philosophical differences arose between the many factions and deep splits became apparent in terms of direction and content. For blacks, the sharpest divisions occurred between two of their standard bearers, Booker T. Washington and W.E.B. Du Bois. Their differences in the philosophy of education would demand center stage among the many conflicting positions. Those differences are the central focus of Chapter 3.

Chapter 2

The Washington/Du Bois Debate

This chapter exposes the deep philosophical rift that occurred in the black community as a result of several political concerns, chief among them the question of black higher education. One faction in this dispute was led by Booker T. Washington, the other by William E. B. Du Bois. The two were extremely different; Washington was the son of a former slave and entered the dispute with a clear knowledge of the hardships that slavery had wrought. Du Bois was a native of Massachusetts, well-educated and born to a family that had escaped the ravages of slavery a century before. Each believed his view was correct and, at times, went to great lengths to assure that others would believe in the efficacy of his position.

The period of American history between the Civil War and World War I, 1865 to 1915, can be studied from many perspectives. An often-overlooked theme is that of Pan-Africanism, a movement in the black community during this period that was aimed at repatriating blacks to their homeland. The repatriationists formed the most radical of black political groups. Their existence threatened not only the philosophies of those who sought accommodation with whites but the goodwill of the northern white philanthropists as well. It became a driving force among many of the intellectuals of the day, who became staunch advocates for the positions held by Marcus Garvey, Alfred Sam, Henry Turner, and others. Henry McNeal Turner, a bishop in the African Methodist Episcopal church, was by far the most articulate of the repatriationists in post-Reconstruction America. He visited Africa in 1891, 1893, 1895, and 1898. Turner saw no chance of manhood for blacks in America (Moses, 1978, p. 201).

Honorary Chief Alfred C. Sam repatriated five dozen blacks to the African Gold Coast in 1914 in a crusade that he claimed had religious significance for blacks. Neither of these men reached as many blacks as the movement of Marcus Garvey, the Jamaican emigré who founded the Universal Negro Improvement Association and the African Communities League. Garvey was able to attract a number of black intellectuals to his cause. Among them were Frederick Douglass; Emmett J. Scott, former secretary to Booker T. Washington; T. Thomas Fortune, who served as editor of the organization journal, *The Negro World*; and William H. Ferris, who was its literary editor. In addition there was Ida B. Wells; J. A. Rogers, the popular historian; Egyptian nationalist Duse Mohamed; and Amy Jaques Garvey, who edited the Spanish edition of the *New World* (Moses, 1978, p. 264).

Pan-Africanism represented the most radical political position taken by blacks. Neither Washington nor Du Bois was part of this movement but both rejected separatism, seeking positions that were thought to be less confrontational. Both were Americans by birth and both sought to remedy the plight of black Americans within the confines of this society.

If one is to study this period under the theme of American black education, the name Booker T. Washington must stand out as the dominant figure of the time. Booker T. Washington was the last of the great black American leaders born a slave who went on to exert a major influence in the sociopolitical life of the twentieth century. He became a major spokesperson for America's black millions.

Washington was born the son of a slave and a white man on a southern plantation in 1856 in southern Virginia. He knew first-hand the tragedies of slavery. When freedom came to Virginia,

Washington (the name he chose for himself), his brother, and his mother migrated to the mining community of Malden, West Virginia. It was in Malden that he was able to receive the raw beginnings of an education. He worked both as a miner and a houseboy during his childhood but never lost sight of education as his primary goal.

At age 17 he left his hometown for Hampton Institute in Virginia. At the time Hampton was a vocational high school that had been founded by the Freedmen's Bureau for the education of blacks. Washington graduated with honors in 1875, but more important was the impression he had made on the director, General Samuel Chapman Armstrong. Five years later when the Hampton's director was asked to nominate someone for the directorship of the new Tuskeegee facility to be built in Alabama, Washington was his choice. This was a most important appointment and should have served as a warning for blacks seeking political and social equality: Armstrong had earned the reputation of a man who never trusted highly educated blacks (Anderson, 1988, p. 57). Armstrong never gained the confidence of those whom he oversaw and represented a class and a world outlook that was opposed to the higher aspirations of the freed men. For Washington to be selected by this man meant that his agendas, both political and social, would not offend.

General Armstrong was not one to encourage the growth of thought that would challenge the traditional inequalities of wealth and power. In the monthly newspaper published at Hampton, Armstrong packaged his conservatism to attract northern white philanthropists. Armstrong advised black leaders to stay out of politics for generations to come (Anderson, 1988, p. 37).

Washington was a product of this highly conservative Hampton philosophy and his work at Tuskeegee showed him to be an avid student. At Tuskeegee, as at Hampton, political activism was not to be found, the economic philosophy that championed the black cause was absent, and the idea that education would move black graduates to a position of parity with whites was not present. Washington opposed black migration to northern states, did not oppose segregated facilities, and viewed his black constituency as "organically weak" (Moses, 1978, p. 96).

At the time of his appointment, Washington was only 25. He started with little more than determination and hope but in ten years Tuskeegee Institute had more than 450 students, fourteen buildings, and over 1400 acres of farmland. Much of this was due to his persuasive fundraising. His success made him a prominent individual in black southern education but that was soon to change.

Washington was the chief proponent of industrial education and designed his school as the temple of that belief. He founded the school in 1881, only sixteen years after Emancipation. Though no one disagreed that industrial education had its place in the lives of black people, there were those who thought that free men should have the right to choose from among the many disciplines, just as their white counterparts had always done. Washington's doctrine, a postulate of accommodation, became the scourge of blacks who saw themselves as equal to all other human beings. The thought that there would be those who would oppose him over the disagreement on rightful place of blacks as citizens, caused Washington to exercise his overwhelming influence over the black community. To insure adherence to his doctrine, he began to dole out political appointments, philanthropic gifts, business opportunities, and jobs (Meier, 1966, p. 181).

In 1895 Washington was asked to speak at the International Exposition in Atlanta, Georgia. On September 18 Washington delivered the address that delineated his philosophy and the road that he would travel in his attempt to secure a better life for black Americans. In that speech he allayed the fears of whites by instructing blacks to be patient and long-suffering in their pursuit of equality. He pledged on behalf of his black brethren a new fidelity, love, and cooperation with southern whites, without seeking the guarantees of civil or constitutional rights. In his address he said,

> We shall stand by you with a devotion that no foreigner can approach, ready to lay down our lives, if need be, in defence of

yours, interlacing our industrial, commercial, civil, and religious life with yours in a way that shall make the interests of both races one. In all things that are purely social we can be as separate as the fingers, yet one as the hand in all things essential to mutual progress. (Moses, 1978, p. 98)

By the time he was finished, whites, who at the outset had been leery of him, applauded enthusiastically.

This speech, often called the Atlanta Compromise, was the launching pad for Washington's meteoric rise to national prominence. President Grover Cleveland sent his personal greeting. He was hailed as the "Black Moses," consulted by congressmen, funded by millionaires, and honored by Harvard University. He entertained and was entertained by the most influential political and social movers of the day.

Washington's acceptance in high places can best be gauged in his 1899 trip abroad. In a three-month trip he was entertained by Queen Victoria, two dukes, and several other members of the British aristocracy. He met James Bryce and Henry Stanley; former president Benjamin Harrison; Archbishop John Ireland; and two justices of the Supreme Court received him at the Peace Conference at the Hague. In addition he received honorary degrees both from Harvard and Dartmouth (Du Bois, 1940, p. 71). From 1901 to 1912 he was the political referee in many federal appointments or actions concerning blacks and in many regarding the white South (Du Bois, 1940, p. 72).

Booker T. Washington had been anointed by the white American power structure as the leading spokesman for blacks on all educational matters. As a result, the media was acceptable, his plan was pushed forward, and he became the acceptable alternative to a more radical fringe group of blacks who were beginning to express disfavor with Washington. His influence grew in terms of black politics, black small business, and the ability to influence white public opinion. Perhaps unwittingly, Washington's rise to power was at a cost to his race that is still being determined. Until his death in 1915, Booker T. Washington remained one of the most powerful men in America (Berry, 1982, p. 274).

Washington's view of justice was buoyed by the acceptance he received in high places of government and society. His campus was visited and praised by the president of the United States. His industrial school concept became the accepted model throughout the world, but his vision for black Americans was shortsighted. In terms of engineering, he forestalled the full-fledged involvement and the resulting development of black engineers by twenty to thirty years. He also condemned bright young minds to vocations beneath their abilities, and for this he was applauded by most Americans.

Washington's methods and his philosophy, when taken to their logical conclusions, were not designed to produce the types of individuals who would compete with whites for jobs or political positions. This would have been disruptive to the calm for which Washington advised blacks to strive. It would certainly not have produced the corps of black engineers that was to come. Rather, blacks would have been relegated to second-class positions in terms of training and vocations. Nevertheless, his doctrine had won him a place in history.

There were those who looked beyond the present. A group of black intellectuals denounced the work of Washington. This group was led by two Harvard graduates, William E. B. Du Bois and William Monroe Trotter. Trotter was the owner of the Boston-based newspaper, *The Guardian*, in which he wrote scathing appraisals of Washington's tactics. Trotter confronted Washington as the Tuskeegean delivered a speech in Boston in 1905 at a meeting of the National Negro Business League. Trotter was arrested as a disruptive person but made the most of this by editorializing in *The Guardian* on what came to be known as the Boston Riot.

This act, the Boston Riot, became the turning point for Du Bois. Du Bois wrote a letter to Trotter, who had been jailed, expressing his disfavor with Washington and his sympathy for Trotter since his incarceration was a clear violation of his civil rights. Trotter published the letter, an act that became the opening of a drama that would last far beyond the death of Booker T. Washington. Du Bois and Washington are a study in sharp contrasts. Du Bois was born in 1868 in Great Barrington, Massachusetts. He graduated from high school in his hometown in 1884 and entered Fisk University. Over the next decade he attended and graduated from Fisk University, Harvard University, and the University of Berlin (Du Bois, 1971, p. 3). In 1905 Trotter and Du Bois formed the Niagara Movement, a political organization dedicated to the continued agitation for civil rights, voting privileges, human rights, and equal education.

At first their opposition to Washington's leadership proved to be ineffective, since their numbers were small and represented only a fraction of the community. Du Bois came to the fight with a distinguished background as an author of articles for the *Atlantic Monthly* and the *World's Work* magazine. He had worked in Georgia to better the living conditions of blacks and to stop discrimination in the distribution of school funds, and he had lobbied the legislature for the elimination of discrimination in railway travel. He had also prepared an exhibition showing the condition of black Americans for the 1900 Paris Exposition, which had won a grand prize. He became a Fellow of the American Association for the Advancement of Science in 1904 after his 1900 acceptance as a member. In fact, on his return to America from his doctoral studies at the University of Berlin, he applied to Tuskeegee for a job.

Between the two men, Washington and Du Bois, there existed some common ground: the recognition of the value of education and a recognition of the necessity of black participation in skilled trades. The controversy that existed between the two came from the basic differences in their approaches to leadership and dominance and their vastly different philosophies regarding black higher education.

Du Bois objected vehemently to the "Tuskeegee Machine," the name given to the structure of organizations, media, and the many groups that formed the Washington constituency. In some cases it was obvious that allegiances were bought. In other cases, groups acquiesced many times out of fear (Franklin, 1982, p. 14).

The Souls of Black Folks, a 1903 work by Du Bois, shows the contempt with which he viewed Booker T. Washington's accommodating position. He pointed to Washington's willingness to submit to black disfranchisement, his complicity in the steady withdrawal of aid from black institutions of higher education, and his unwillingness to address the problems of civil rights (Meier, 1980, p. 37).

Those involved in the Niagara Movement regarded Washington as a puppet of the white power structure. It was well known that in addition to white philanthropists, a large section of the black press and powerful white southern politicians were deeply involved in Washington's movement. By the time the Niagara Movement was mobilized, Washington's influence had spread such that few black federal appointments were made without his input. This was true not only of the few black appointments but often the white appointments as well. Tuskeegee Institute became the center for black information, a "national bureau of black information."

Much of this activity was financed by northern whites. Their goal was to discourage black political participation and to develop a strong labor force that would offset the white unionized labor that was beginning to appear in the North. Next, the task of the machine was to hammer into submission and conformity the black intelligentsia. This would prove to be a formidable task for Washington, but with money and the help of whites the task seemed reasonable (Anderson, 1988, p. 106).

Unlike Washington, Du Bois was not a favorite of the southern conservatives. Nor was he to be silenced. His continuing battles with Washington over the direction that black leadership should take became as great a battle within the race as the black/white struggle between the races.

The years between 1900 and 1910 brought to the surface the sharp differences that existed within the race. Washington's work had stifled the forward progress of blacks who did not agree with him and by so doing, robbed the black community and the nation of economic opportunities that would have been beneficial. His zeal for the task often caused him to use underhanded schemes against his opponents. On occasions he hired Pinkerton detectives to spy on Niagara members; at other times he attempted to infiltrate their movement and if someone openly opposed him, as one newspaperman did, Washington had the power to destroy his or her career (Franklin, 1982, p. 14).

There was also a side to Booker T. Washington that went without public acclaim even though the stances he took at these times were positions that, even today, deserve praise. While locked in combat with his critics, Washington fought several race battles in which his name was never used. One of these was a legal case in which a black was held on a peonage charge. Due to Washington's intervention the case was won and the law declared unconstitutional. The lawyer in this case was secretly financed by Washington. In other instances he financed cases to overturn a ruling that disenfranchised blacks but lost at the Supreme Court level on technicalities. In these and other instances his involvement was always hidden for fear that it might prejudice his appeal with northern philanthropists (Franklin, 1982, p. 13).

As students of black history look back, with the wisdom of the intervening years, it becomes clear that the ongoing struggle between Washington and Du Bois is one of the great battles of black existence in America. Those who can now appreciate the strides made by blacks in terms of their constitutional guarantees realize that both men had flawed images of the black American.

For the first time since arriving on these shores, spokesmen of national prominence declared the worth of their race. To observant blacks, this meant that a new sense of self-worth would be one of the fruitful outcomes of this struggle. Du Bois' assessment of black worth challenged the status quo while Washington's was compliant. Few philanthropists agreed with Du Bois; many agreed with Washington. As a result, Washington's ascendancy was complete (Berry, 1982, p. 274).

For young black people who wished to become engineers, medical doctors, or other types of professionals, the way was blocked. For although the philanthropists gave money to the Washington project at Tuskeegee, Washington and those who appointed him never insisted on equal status, equal primary and secondary education, fair and equitable distribution of public funds, or accreditation of the postsecondary programs. They did not even ask that the graduates be sent north to take positions in industries.

Du Bois, on the other hand, gave hope and inspiration to a group of blacks who wished to strive for goals beyond those prescribed by whites. Engineering, medicine, dentistry, and business were some of the spheres of education thought to be beyond the grasp of blacks, but they were goals to which Du Bois devoted a lifetime of work. Du Bois introduced a new term into the language, "Talented Tenth." The term designated that small percentage of blacks who were endowed with the talents and brains to lead the race to self-sufficiency. The idea that Du Bois could fashion a scheme that excluded 90 percent of black America was taken as an affront by many of his followers. He insisted that a college-trained elite could lift the lower class, an elitist plan that was as offensive as any accommodationist idea advanced by Washington.

Washington gave credence to the widespread belief of that era that blacks were inferior. The more Washington was praised, the more strident Du Bois became in his opposition to Washington's doctrine. So adamant was Du Bois about the entire race issue that he, along with others of similar persuasion, formed the very radical (for that time) National Association for the Advancement of Colored People (NAACP) (Aptheker, 1951, p. 876).

The ultimate example of the societal misuse of Booker T. Washington came when the northern philanthropists used him as the conduit for much of the money that was to be dispersed among the small black southern industrial schools, thereby assuring that southern black educational leaders were kept in line (Enck, 1976, p. 79). As a result of this funneling, Washington's school had a permanent endowment of more than $1,800,000 in 1912 (*Crisis*, November 1912, p. 34). This was the largest endowment of any black school and larger than that of many white institutions of the day. Much of this endowment had come as a result of a $600,000 gift given to the school by Washington's friend, Andrew Carnegie (Du Bois, 1940, p. 72).

This battle took place while the nation underwent the most severe racial clash in its history, and while turn-of-the-century southern politicians like "Pitchfork" Ben Tillman declared they wanted no Negro to vote—not even men like Booker T. Washington—and Governor James K. Vardaman of Mississippi declared that "God created the Negro for a menial" (Hughes, 1968, p. 244). It was also a time of extreme legislative and judicial repression: legalized peonage laws, Jim Crow laws for public accommodations, and disenfranchisement. In spite of the turmoil, blacks persevered. Many colleges were opened by white philanthropists for blacks between 1865 and World War I (Bowles, 1971, 298). Among them are many of the colleges referred to today under the umbrella of the United Negro Colleges.

In the end, Washington returned to Tuskeegee to live out his years while Du Bois became the new focal point of black striving. And though others may measure the men against different standards, black engineering students know that the first black engineers to graduate from black schools came from Howard University, North Carolina Agricultural and Technical College, and Hampton Institute, not Tuskeegee.

The anger and discord that came as a result of the Washington–Du Bois battle meant that blacks were becoming interested, not only in the men, but in the idea of choice in educational format. For most black Americans this option had never been available. Washington's industrial education had appeal for those who were not ready to meet the challenge of the real world, while Du Bois' Talented Tenth held out promise for others. Collectively they are responsible for the new black interest in all of education. The next chapter will explore some of the consequences of this renewed interest and the reactions of the greater society to the interest.

Chapter 3

Educational Opportunity and the Development of Black Institutions

EDUCATIONAL OPPORTUNITIES, 1900–1930

Prior to World War I few opportunities existed for blacks to work in engineering fields and few blacks with the required expertise. The 10 percent of the black population that lived outside the South might find opportunities for the necessary education, but those living within the states of the Old Confederacy had little hope of such an outcome. During the first three decades of the twentieth century many converging attitudes and events became more apparent and their combined effect meant that social justice and black collegiate education were at risk. This was true nationally but in the South it had extreme consequences. If we were going to produce technologically trained black people, we needed schools with classical curricula. At the turn of the century the pool of black teachers for southern public schools was desperately low. The ratio was 1 teacher to every 93 black children of school age (Anderson, 1988, p. 111). The number of white missionaries that had once staffed the schools of ex-slaves during the post–Civil War era had greatly diminished. This vacuum caused by the lack of qualified teachers for black children became an area of heated debate. An ideological battle raged among northern industrial philanthropists, northern missionaries, black leaders, and the white southern power structure.

Each group understood that the corps of black teachers needed to staff black schools was the key to the transmission of values and, ultimately, a way of life. Northern industrial philanthropists were quick to form an alliance with those institutions that represented the Hampton-Tuskeegee ideology. They wanted manual and industrial training as the basis of the curriculum (Weinberg, 1977, p. 269). A fund was established by the General Education Board to underwrite many of the operational costs of schools that fell into this category. Northern missionaries, fewer than in earlier years, were torn between the industrial model and the classical liberal curriculum. Black leaders, with some notable exceptions, believed the classical curriculum offered blacks a greater list of options in what they believed to be a new era. The white southern establishment gave no indication of caring for either system. As a result, southern state schools were underfunded and grossly inadequate. In fact, if all school-aged black children had wished to enroll in the years prior to 1920, there would not have been sufficient schools in which to house them (Anderson, 1988, p. 110).

With this type of wrangling over the direction in which black education should head and with the accompanying poor funding, many black children were miseducated or not educated at all (Weinberg, 1977, p. 59). These children represented the collegiate aspirants that should have been produced for college entrance from 1925 to 1940. Engineers, technologically trained graduates, businesspeople, doctors, and many other would-be professionals were lost to the black community because no southern state provided the basic tools of education.

Many black private institutions were greatly influenced by the financial support of northern philanthropists. Since these institutions relied on donations for their annual budget, many were forced to subscribe to the manual training philosophy for their survival. In cases where presidents and headmasters refused to submit to outside influences, many were removed. In Fort Valley, Georgia, an independent school had been founded by John W. Davison in 1890. Fort Valley High and Industrial School (the name was changed in 1932 to Fort Valley Normal and Industrial School and to Fort Valley State College in 1939) received no funds from the state of Georgia and depended on donations and tuitions for its existence. Davison was removed from his post as president during the 1903–1904 school year by the General Education Board. At the root of his dismissal was Davison's refusal to abandon a liberal curriculum for the school. When he was dismissed, those who sympathized with his position on the school's educational direction were also dismissed. The board of trustees was purged of all black members and replaced by blacks who more closely identified with the intentions of the General Education Board. To be certain that the school would not "slip back" the Board insisted on a white man to head the school's Board of Trustees. With these alterations, the school could receive a liberal funding from the General Education Board (Anderson, 1988, p. 115).

In another such case in 1903, Richard R. Wright, Sr. was president of Georgia State Industrial College, where the curriculum emphasized academic education and training in skilled trades. His refusal to alter the course of his institution meant that the Georgia State Industrial College was not among those schools receiving grants from the General Education Board (Anderson, 1988, p. 122).

By 1920, with civil rights at their lowest point since the Civil War and with race relations suffering under the weight of overtly racist acts, many black citizens were convinced that their worth to the country was minimal. This was shortly after World War I and at a time when many racist organizations were again gaining strength in both northern and southern communities.

Between 1914 and 1924 a concentrated effort by the NAACP for racial tolerance was waged that inflamed white opposition (Du Bois, 1940, p. 193). The backlash by whites to black political activism, combined with the refusal of the federal government to act responsibly, led to grave doubts and fear in the black community. Even black participation in the war took on a demeaning cast. Blacks were allowed to serve in the Navy only as messboys and were barred entirely from the Marine Corps. The Army accepted blacks as enlisted men but had no intention of commissioning them as officers. Only the agitation of the NAACP and a group of prominent white citizens reversed the Army's decision. As a result, an officers' training installation was built near Des Moines, Iowa, and in October 1917, 639 black men were commissioned with ranks ranging from second lieutenant to captain (Meier, 1966, p. 193).

A tale often told during the twenties and current even in my own childhood tells with wizened humor the plight of the early twentieth-century black. It tells of a cold, wet, and hungry black who appeals to the Lord for deliverance. He is advised by the Lord to "Go back to Mississippi." The black then asks if there are alternatives, to which the Lord repeats "Go back to Mississippi." The black migrant, now deathly afraid, asks, "Lord will you go with me?" to which the Lord replies, "As far as Cincinnati."

A joke, to be sure, but it conveys accurately the life of fear that the least of the black population lived. In 1917 race riots had occurred in Philadelphia and Chester, Pennsylvania, and East St. Louis, Illinois. Thirty-nine blacks were killed in these riots, yet no arrests were made (Meier, 1968, p. 192). During the summer of 1919 over twenty race riots erupted from Washington, D.C., west to Chicago and as far south as Elaine, Arkansas, and Longview, Texas (Meier, 1968, p. 194). Those who dared to rise above the status of the common person or to rebel against the racial tyranny of the twenties faced the most severe reactions from the white community.

Still, there were those who sought a college education. In 1914 Howard University graduated the largest class of black students in its history, sixty-eight (*Crisis*, July 1914, p. 15). In that year black colleges in the South graduated an additional 200 young people (*Crisis*, July 1914, p. 15). Equally noteworthy was the fact that many young blacks had opted for formerly all-white schools of the North. In 1913, three black students had graduated as engineers from formerly all-white institutions: D. N. Crosthwaith and H. M. Taylor, both from Purdue University; and James Arthur Dunn, the first black to graduate as an engineer from Ohio State (*Crisis*, July 1913, p. 114–16). Among the black graduates of 1914 were four young engineering graduates: Thomas Bailey of Clark University; Harvey A. Turner, a civil engineer from Rhode Island College; Elmer Cheeks, an electrical engineer from Purdue University; and Daniel D. Fowler, who graduated as a mining engineer from Case (*Crisis*, July 1914, p. 16).

These seven young men followed in the mold set by Lawrence DeWitt Simmons, a 1906 graduate of Yale University's Sheffield Scientific School. Simmons was a native of New Orleans and had attended Talladega College in Alabama, graduating in 1903. He immediately applied to and was accepted at the Sheffield School from which he graduated three years later, thus receiving his bachelor's degree in engineering after a combined seven years of study. After graduation, he was employed by the General Electric Company at its Schenectady, New York, plant where he remained for more than ten years (*Crisis*, April 1914, p. 42).

Nearly all black engineering graduates of this time had been forced to attend northern colleges to obtain their engineering degrees. If they were fortunate enough to have had the proper preparation—a bachelor's degree from a black institution with two or three years' study in science or math—then the northern college stay might be as short as an additional three years; for most, it would be an additional four or five years. If, however, they were the products of inadequate or unaccredited southern preparatory education systems, the degree could take as long as an additional seven or eight years. As a result, the completion of each degree was the result of a tremendous investment of time, effort, and money.

Although they were admitted to northern institutions, most black applicants were discouraged from entering these institutions in subtle ways. As an example of the tactics used by institutions of higher learning, an inquiry from a black 1914 applicant to the Ohio State School of Engineering received the following response:

> I should be very glad to aid you in any way possible in securing an education in Electrical Engineering. I regret to say, however, that I have nothing at my disposal for your encouragement. There is no

objection to your coming to Ohio State University and entering any
course for which you are qualified. Every year we have a number
of young people of both sexes of the Negro race who attend the
University without embarrassment or hindrance. The way is entirely open so far as that is concerned, and I shall be glad to be of
any assistance to you in my power. On one matter, however, I feel
constrained to say just a word. The sentiment north of the Ohio
River seems to be persistent against the Negro in skilled labor that
I doubt very much whether an educated Negro has a fair show or a
show worthwhile in this part of the country. (*Crisis*, July 1914, pp.
128–29)

For those blacks who were admitted to northern institutions,
their stay was often troubled. Discrimination in housing and other
forms of social isolation were common. Blacks were also barred
from the collegiate engineering societies, a group in which membership traditionally was the first step toward professional affilia-
tion. If they graduated, they were then barred from professional
engineering societies, the organizations that secured positions, set
standards, and generally spoke for the profession (Einberg, 1977,
p. 290).

One of the early black architectural engineering graduates of
Drexel Institute of Philadelphia, Sidney Pittman, fought discrimination throughout his career. Sidney Pittman was born in Montgomery, Alabama, in 1875. In 1892 he entered Tuskeegee Institute
and graduated in 1897. He moved to Philadelphia and entered
Drexel Institute, graduating as an honor student in 1900. Pittman
returned to Alabama to accept a position at Tuskeegee Institute as
its resident architect. Among the buildings he designed were the
Y.M.C.A. building in Washington, D.C.; two state normal-school
structures in Frankfort, Kentucky; and buildings on the campus of
Voorhees Industrial School, Denmark, South Carolina. The National Training School in Durham, North Carolina, gave him a
contract for eight buildings. He secured a federal government
contract to design the Negro Building for the Jamestown Exposition at Norfolk, Virginia. He also designed the Garfield public
school building in Washington, D.C.; the Carnegie Library in

Houston, Texas; the Hall for the United Brothers of Friendship in San Antonio; and the Grand Temple of the State Grand Lodge, Knights of Pythias, in Dallas. All are buildings used extensively by blacks. Yet even as the son-in-law of the great Booker T. Washington, Pittman could not secure contracts for buildings with mixed-race usage. It is doubtful that he would have been awarded many contracts had it not been for his familial connection. Stories such as this help one to understand the duplicity of the system: on the one hand allowing a black man to complete the required education, then limiting the use of the end product of that expertise, primarily to black consumers. Nevertheless, Pittman's work stands today as testimony of his early contribution.

William Cook, a native of Greenville, South Carolina, was educated at Claflin University and taught mechanical arts there and at Georgia State College. Cook attended Massachusetts Institute of Technology for postgraduate studies, after which he sat for the federal government examination for senior draftsman. In 1908 he was assigned to supervise the erection and completion of the post offices in Lancaster, Pennsylvania, and Ashland, Ohio. Cook was the second black man to hold the position of senior draftsman in the federal system (the first was Lowell W. Baker) (*Crisis*, May 1917, p. 31). Cook's work on the Lancaster, Pennsylvania, post office was one of the first projects overseen by a black man that was designed for mixed-race usage.

In each of these cases the engineer attended a black college and then went on to attend a white school that had an accredited engineering program. There were no accredited black programs in 1915 and this fact is important since white schools could determine the number and the identity of black engineers. It also meant that those blacks who were admitted usually arrived with superb transcripts and impressive letters of recommendation. As an example, between 1900 and 1914 four black students graduated from the prestigious Sheffield School, the engineering school of Yale University. They were John Taylor Williams (1900), William Miller Thorne, Jr. (1906), Lawrence DeWitt Simmons (1906), and James Weldon Queenan (1906). The Yale Archival Collection lists aca-

Table 1
Total Black College Graduates, 1914–1929

Year	Total Number	Total/Northern
1914	267	not available
1915	281	38
1916	338	not available
1917	445	77
1918	396	175
1919	373	53
1920	364	100
1921	461	not available
1922	523	77
1923	517	129
1924	523	183
1925	not available	not available
1926	1000+	293
1927	1100+	261
1928	1277	339
1929	1591	394

Source: This chart is a compilation of graduation reports from *Crisis* magazine, May through August, 1914 through 1929.

demic preparation as part of each student's biography. Williams attended Andover Academy, Thorne attended the Mount Hermon School, and Simmons had attended Talladega College (Yale Archives, Sheffield School Histories).

In 1915 and 1916 five additional black engineers were graduated from northern schools: Charles A. Tribbett from Yale University; J. C. Webster from the University of Pennsylvania; W. H. Steward from Armour Institute; C. H. Burch from Ohio State; and E. A. Brown from the University of Illinois (*Crisis*, July 1915, p. 137; *Crisis*, July 1916, pp. 119–27). The production of black college graduates, engineers included, was beginning to spiral upward just as the nation entered the war. Bright young men went to war and the effect of their patriotism was felt in the graduation statistics of 1918, 1919, and 1920.

For black college students in those years an examination of the June, July, and August issues of black publications from 1914 to 1929 produces the following graduation statistics. This fifteen-year span was chosen because definite records exist from at least two schools—Howard University and the Massachusetts Institute of Technology—that fully cover this period and that can be used as comparisons. The statistics show the total of black graduates for any given year and the portion of the total that graduated from northern schools (Table 1).

Darnley Howard was one of those who did not serve in the Army. Instead, in 1920, he became the first black engineering graduate of the Polytechnic Institute (Rensselaer) in Troy, New York (Allison, July 1920, p. 126). He later accepted a position on the faculty of the Howard University School of Engineering.

The annual graduation records show that during this fifteen-year span, 1914 to 1929, sixty-seven black engineers were graduated from only two of the many existing programs of the day—thirty-one from MIT and an additional thirty-six from Howard University. These, plus others coming from the limited number of schools that accepted blacks, and the probability that only a small number would be eligible since adequate preparatory programs did not exist, suggest that perhaps 400 may have been produced during this fifteen-year period. Four hundred is a good estimate since the 1930 census showed 500 black engineers and architects living in America.

Thus, the record shows that minority engineers were being produced, but the evidence of their acceptance as fully prepared coworkers on a national scale was slight. The tone had been set by President Woodrow Wilson, who made great promises to blacks during his campaign. So convincing was he that W.E.B. Du Bois spoke positively of his sincerity. Once elected Wilson changed dramatically. His passion for democracy and self-determination was confined to caucasians of European descent; he eliminated nearly all of the black patronage jobs; and he ordered the segregation of the District of Columbia. For engineering hopefuls, he segregated the federal bureaucracy, severely limiting opportunities for blacks to work for government agencies (Morris, 1975, p. 193).

Education, the usual refuge for educated blacks of the day, had an overabundance of black technical types working in positions beneath their educational preparation. But when we look at the few black collegiate institutions that had reason to call for their services it is obvious that there was a disincentive for blacks to pursue the technologies. South of the Mason-Dixon line their acceptance was further hindered by the racial climate and restrictive union membership rules.

The period between 1910 and 1930 was particularly pivotal, not only in the development of black engineering education but in terms of the overall philosophy of black higher education in this country. During these years accreditation of black schools, poor state funding, union bias, insufficient elementary and secondary schools, and lack of community control combined to pose a severe threat to forward movement in black higher education.

Fortunately there were voices that continued to rail against the inequities. The years between 1910 and 1930 were not years of dynamic change but rather a time of gradual shift in focus in black higher education. These were also years of growing self-determination (Anderson, 1988, pp. 267–68).

THE TWENTIES

Fisk University had been chosen as the capstone of black private postsecondary education and northern industrial philanthropists plotted a strategy to gain control over the institution. This was accomplished with the help of black accommodationists and the Nashville Commercial Club, which included Tennessee's governor and the mayor of Nashville. Promises of millions of dollars in endowments and gifts to eliminate the college's indebtedness were part of the lure.

Meanwhile a white president, Fayette Avery McKenzie, had been appointed by the General Education Board. The board of trustees had been "reorganized" in 1920 removing all non-accommodationist blacks and replacing them with manual training ideologues. The decision was made to alter the liberal curriculum of the college to more closely resemble that of both Hampton and Tuskeegee (Anderson, 1988, p. 263).

McKenzie disbanded the student government association, forbade student dissent, and suspended the *Fisk Herald*, the oldest student publication among black colleges. He refused to allow an NAACP chapter to be established on the campus and had the librarian remove radical articles from NAACP literature. New stringent rules of conduct were imposed, and dancing and hand-holding were forbidden on the assumption that "blacks are particularly sensuous beings" (Anderson, 1988, p. 268). McKenzie insisted on complete separation of the races even though he hired whites to teach at the all-black school (Anderson, 1988, p. 268). In 1924, following many articles in the journals of black America, W.E.B. Du Bois, a Fisk alumnus, was invited as the commencement speaker. The speech was highly critical of the Fisk administration. It enflamed the student body, which found in Du Bois a leader who spoke without fear about their dissatisfaction. Fisk alumni, community organizations, students, and black leaders mounted a campaign that unseated McKenzie in 1925 (Anderson, 1988, p. 268).

Despite the resounding repudiation of the manual training philosophy at Hampton and Tuskeegee, white industrialists continued to support it. Proof of the failure of this ideology was seen in the changes that took place at Hampton Institute during the twenties. Though Hampton's enrollment remained stable at between 1000 and 1100, the college division grew from 21 students in 1920 to 417 in 1927. By 1929 applicants for admission had to be high school graduates.

This decade also saw a return of blatantly racist attitudes toward the limited integration of southern black college teaching staffs. Northern whites who had gone to teach in black southern schools of higher education had been forced out and replaced by a corps of intolerant white southern instructors. At schools that should have been in the forefront of the battle for technological education, racist ideas were stifling any attempt at expansion.

At Fisk, southern white instructors, who were rapidly replacing black staff, often refused to acknowledge their black colleagues and at one point not a dean or head of a department was black; at Lincoln University in Pennsylvania the teaching staff consisted of white professors, and at Hampton severe racial unrest existed (Du

Bois, 1971, p. 542). The emphasis at this point had to be on the preservation of these institutions and as a result, blacks were forced to make compromises that were not in their best interests.

In spite of this bleak outlook, a new organization, the National Technical Association, was founded in the mid-1920s. Membership was limited to blacks with a degree in engineering or architecture plus five years experience in the field. Obviously the membership was never large, but by 1937 the national organization boasted more than 200 members.

The organization was formed to foster the development of engineering opportunities for blacks and to expand the limited job market that black engineers faced. The association assisted in the retention of the College of Engineering and Architecture at Howard University; engaged in the placement of black engineers with municipal, state, and federal agencies; and agitated for more accommodation for blacks in the private sector (Daniel, 1937, p. 662).

In contrast to the American experience, McGill University Engineering School of Canada hired George F. Albergu as a member of its faculty in 1921. Albergu, a Jamaican, was educated at Jamaica's Monroe College and awarded a Jamaican scholarship of $3,000 with which he entered McGill in 1911. He won the Mathematics prize in 1913 and graduated from the McGill School of Engineering in 1915.

After graduation he worked as chief inspector in the munitions department of Cement County, Canada; for three years was a member of the Expeditionary Construction Battalion; and spent a year in the office of the chief engineer of the Canadian Railway (*Crisis*, January 1922, pp. 301–02).

The twenties saw movement in the black community toward greater self-determination. The ousting of McKenzie at Fisk came after ten years in office. The repudiation of the manual training philosophy as the chief expression of black higher education came after a long and costly intrarace struggle. Both of these situations illustrate the vulnerability of black higher education in the early decades of the twentieth century. Fisk, as an example of the best in black postsecondary institutions, could be intimidated by the lure of an endowment. This also shows the extent to which outsiders, northern industrialists, directed the course of black education. The establishment of the National Technical Association must be seen as an extremely bright accomplishment, one that, ten years earlier, would have been impossible. This trend toward self-reliance would continue in the 1930s.

THE THIRTIES

The thirties presented a confusing set of options for black students wishing to go beyond high school. During the thirties, many of the colleges and universities that would later become open institutions were still practicing restrictive admissions. Though they did not openly admit this policy, white parents could be sure that if they sent their children to certain schools there would be no black students. This was true at northern schools such as Princeton University; Mills College (California); George Washington University; Worcester Polytechnic; Vassar; Swarthmore College; and most Catholic Schools, such as Catholic University, Holy Cross, and Notre Dame (*Crisis*, August 1931, p. 262).

Other northern schools allowed blacks to attend but would not permit them to live in the dormitories. There were over fifty such schools. Included among them were Ohio University, Bryn Mawr College, Bucknell University, Southern California, Villanova, Whittier College, Washington and Jefferson College, Wittenberg College, Colorado College, Indiana University, Kansas State College, Knox College, Temple University, the University of Arizona, the University of Cincinnati, the University of Kansas, the University of Oregon, and the University of Michigan (*Crisis*, August 1931, p. 162).

During the long struggle for fair and equal treatment by accrediting organizations and engineering societies, black colleges, despite their lack of recognition, continued to produce young men and women of substance. It became quite clear that limited admissions to existing schools of engineering and the inability of black institutions to underwrite new engineering programs meant that only a fraction of deserving students would ever become engineers, if the 1900–1930 pattern continued.

In terms of accreditation, those organizations with the power to approve black colleges were usually white and opposed viewing black schools as the equals of traditional white colleges. Often the persons on boards of accreditation were from schools that did not accept blacks as students. This fact alone caused deep and unsettling dissatisfaction in the black educational community. Volumes have been written on the circuitous routes taken to avoid black collegiate accreditation. The 1930 census showed that of the 200,000 engineers in America, about 500 were blacks—this at a time when blacks comprised 10 percent of the population. It also revealed that there were 66,000 engineering and architectural students, of whom approximately 100 were black. Thirty-one, nearly one-third of these students, attended Howard University, with smaller but significant numbers attending the Massachusetts Institute of Technology, Cornell University, Rensselaer Polytechnic Institute, Ohio State University, the University of Pennsylvania, the University of Pittsburgh, the University of Michigan, the University of Illinois, the University of Wisconsin, and Armour Institute of Technology (Downing, June 1935, p. 63). Each attendee represents a significant achievement for the 1930s.

At the time of this census, there were over 150 schools of engineering and architecture, but still no fully accredited or "recognized" school on a black campus. If, in the late twenties, a more accepting attitude had prevailed in which black students had felt welcome at all institutions, the fact that a black school had not been accredited would not have been as pivotal in the developments that were to follow. Schools of engineering might have developed that recruited the finest students to build a new reality. Instead the threat to educational attainment posed by the racial barriers meant that if blacks did not control their own institutions, they could never expect to rise to technological parity.

There was no lack of interest in engineering among black men of high school age. In 1930 Ralph Bullock, by use of a questionnaire, canvassed nearly 2000 black high school males concerning their career choices. The questionnaires went to students in North Carolina, Tennessee, Georgia, Virginia, Missouri, and the District of Columbia, all with segregated school systems. These were systems where young men had the least hope of going to professional schools. The investigation revealed that medicine was the first choice for a professional career, engineering was fifth, and architecture was twelfth. Many never achieved their goals but the survey showed that blacks were aware of the engineering profession and had aspirations for inclusion (*Crisis*, July 1922, pp. 301–03).

By 1931 more than 18,000 blacks were enrolled in colleges throughout the United States (*Crisis*, August 1931, pp. 261–62). About 10 percent of them were enrolled in predominantly white institutions, but this figure tends to point up the lack of access for blacks rather than the degree to which American colleges welcomed this new population. The majority of blacks who attended northern colleges during the thirties were there on "state scholarships." They came from areas of the country that did not permit blacks to attend local public and private colleges within their states, whether graduate or undergraduate.

The state scholarship was an innovation that originated in the twenties and came into vogue during the thirties as a means of legally extending the segregated status of higher education. States that did not provide professional higher education for blacks made available a limited number of vouchers for blacks to study out of state. In Tennessee the voucher read,

> The scholarship herein provided for shall be granted to the nearest university or institution of learning which the recipient can lawfully attend and which offers educational facilities equal to those of the University of Tennessee, whether such university or institution is located in Tennessee or elsewhere. (Cox, 1940, p. 24)

The genesis of the state scholarship program was the 1924 Missouri state law that provided monies for black collegians to enroll at universities in adjacent states. By doing so the legislature would ensure that the state institutions would remain all-white. Beginning in 1929 Missouri made biennial appropriations from $5,000 to $15,000 for tuition aid. Kentucky, Maryland, Oklahoma, Tennessee, Virginia, and West Virginia followed Missouri in providing the means to keep their state institutions white (Johnson, 1970, p. 181).

The voucher program, with all its racist overtones, was still more than some southern states would provide. As late as 1939 Alabama, Arkansas, Delaware, Florida, Mississippi, and South Carolina had made no provision for out-of-state black collegiate attendance (Johnson, 1943, pp. 180–81). During the eighteen-year period between the Missouri law that provided vouchers for blacks was enacted and 1939, when six southern states were still without programs, over 80 percent of black Americans resided in the South (Smythe, 1976, p. 164). As a result, any ruling affecting the educational opportunity of southern blacks had a monumental effect on black education throughout the country.

This type of denial of access meant that in states that provided the vouchers, black Americans would have to travel beyond state boundaries to receive the education that whites were provided in their home state. In those states where no vouchers were provided, no technological training for blacks existed and as a result, the probability of ever becoming an engineer or a technologically trained black person was extremely remote. Over 3,750,000 black Americans lived in the six states providing no funds for black collegians (Anderson, 1988, p. 41).

Oliver Cox, in his treatise on the inherent inequality in these voucher systems, said this:

> A good college at home has the advantage of advertising education in the community and thus making it desirable to a larger percentage of the population. To many persons, there are cultural, sentimental, and hidden economic problems connected with the business of migrating to the North for an education. These problems may not always be solved by the payment of specified differential tuition and cost of living. (*Crisis*, October 1933, p. 25)

This meant that most blacks in America, regardless of aptitude, were excluded from professional education because the scholarships were few and not all states with segregated higher education provided them (Cox, 1940, p. 25). In Maryland, if a black wanted to become an engineer, he would have to apply and qualify for an out-of-state scholarship. This meant he would be allowed to attend a professional school in the nearest state willing to accept him in that discipline. As a result, Ohio State University, because it bordered many of the southern states, had a black enrollment greater than 50 percent of the black colleges during the thirties, while Columbia University became the haven for those southern teachers who wanted to further their training in that field. No southern state before 1930 provided an in-state engineering education for black aspirants, and between 1930 and 1940 only North Carolina, Washington, D.C., and West Virginia made the provision (Jenkins, 1940, p. 243). This denial, more than any inability on the part of blacks, meant that this decade would again limit the production of black engineers. It also meant that for decades to come blacks would regard this period as a time of educational despair.

The book *One Third of a Nation* is a series of reports from Lorena Hickock, the federal government's confidential investigator, to Harry Hopkins, the president's domestic advisor, during the Great Depression. Her recounting gives some insight into the stance taken by the government toward the plight of minorities during the thirties. In her May 4, 1934, report from Phoenix, Arizona, Hickock reported that in the midst of a crippling depression the government had imposed a two-tiered welfare system that she says was subpar for white people but more than adequate for blacks and Mexican Americans. At the time she was aware that this dual system gave a larger monthly allotment to white recipients than to blacks or Mexican Americans. She based that assumption on her assessment of the unemployment and seeming idleness of the black and Mexican residents of the area. As if to offer an apology she goes on to say that Mexicans and blacks "can't get work." If they were to apply for and receive employment while a white man remained unemployed, "there would be hell to pay" (Lowitt, 1981, pp. 238–39). In other words, the unemployment of blacks and Mexican Americans was more acceptable, more natural, to her eyes.

One may view this as an isolated incident in 1934 related by Ms. Hickock or one can understand that the crop of young people who should have been available to the educational system of our nation two decades later had been seriously neglected and consequently damaged by government policy, racial bigotry, and Ms. Hickock's myopic view.

It is clear that much of the momentum gained during the twenties was dampened by the Depression of the thirties. The diversion of scarce funds from programs that might have been beneficial to the black community and various governmental policies worked to curtail the progress of blacks during the decade. The introduction and acceptance of the voucher system rather than the open access to previously all-white institutions meant that few black college aspirants would benefit from this program. The good college far from home was not the same as the good college within one's state boundary.

The optimism felt at the end of the twenties was being replaced by a confusing set of signals. Northern schools were accepting blacks but not allowing them to stay on campus. Some southern states did not provide vouchers and severe job discrimination was prevalent. Still the numbers of black college students increased.

But as the thirties ended and the national stance became more assured, new opportunities for all Americans would surface. Many of those opportunities were connected to the war effort. If there was to be a concerted drive for black technological inclusion, it should have taken place during the 1940s.

THE FORTIES

The forties brought new blacks into the engineering and technological fields. Defense programs demanded that a larger role be played by all citizens. This was not without opposition from entrenched racists both north and south. Skilled trades, in all but a few instances, were closed to blacks (Johnson, 1970, p. 105). At the Charleston, South Carolina, navy yard black employees trained their white coworkers to serve as engineers in the engine room. Despite their superior experience blacks were never allowed to be engineers. The mechanics' union denied them membership.

The Southern Welding Institute in Memphis prepared 180 blacks as welders, but despite the heavy demand for their skill, they could not get jobs unless they relocated. By 1943 the population of Mobile, Alabama, had doubled to 200,000, with a 30 percent black presence. At government insistence the Alabama Dry Dock and Shipbuilding Company (ADDSCO) upgraded to welders twelve of the more than 7,000 blacks, who held the most menial jobs. They were amply qualified, yet they were assigned to the night shift in an effort to mask their presence. As a result of this move a riot ensued in which more than forty blacks were injured. The company instituted a plan in which black welders and laborers were segregated from their white coworkers (Goldfield, 1990, p. 35).

Interest in many fields of specialization is often sparked by a parent's knowledge and familiarity with that field. In these instances black fathers who might have directed their sons and daughters toward technical fields were dissuaded by the racial climate.

With the war came a new demand for housing throughout the nation. This would mean that black architects would have an opportunity to design large housing developments intended for black residents. Among those who rose to prominence during this period was Hillyard Robinson. Robinson was an architect of unusual ability who for thirteen years served as professor and chairman of the School of Architecture at Howard University. In 1926 his design was chosen for the historic restaurant in the Henry Hudson Hotel in Troy, New York. In 1927 he received the first, second, and fourth prizes offered by the professional journal *Architecture.*

He was appointed by Federal Works Administrator John Carmody as consulting architect to design a large 250-unit housing development just beyond the Washington, D.C., city limits. Robinson's task was to render complete plans and architectural services to the point of construction including site plans and dwelling designs. Robinson had previously designed the Langston Terrace and Frederick Douglass housing developments in Washington, D.C., both of which were seen as "breakthrough" designs in the field of public housing. He had also designed Cook Hall at Howard University. On the Cook Hall project, Robinson used the expertise of the Howard faculty and engineering students (*Crisis*, September 1941, p. 298).

In the same year, 1941, a $300,000 hospital for the city of Newport News, Virginia, was designed by another black architect, William H. Moses, acting chairman of the Hampton Institute building construction department (*Crisis*, October 1941, p. 308).

The decade of the forties, though similar in many ways to those preceding it, provided black engineering hopefuls with new opportunities. It was also the decade of the first great black American commercial engineer, Archie Alexander. His success symbolized a new black engineering advancement that was becoming a reality.

Yet while such opportunities were broadening, there were those that remained closed. Yancey Williams, a Howard University engineering student, filed suit on January 17, 1941, in a District of Columbia court in order to compel the War Department to consider his application for enlistment in the United States Air Corps. He was represented by a lawyer for the National Association for the Advancement of Colored People (NAACP), Thurgood Marshall.

At twenty-four, Williams was a senior mechanical engineering student employed as a technician in Howard University's power plant. He had successfully completed the primary and secondary civilian aeronautics courses and held a private pilot's license. He had also passed the physical examination given to incoming flight cadets. Williams had been recommended by Edward S. Hope, superintendent of buildings and grounds at the university; William T. Courtney, chief engineer of the power plant; and L. K. Downing,

Dean of the School of Engineering. The official reply from the Army was as follows:

Dear Sir,

Receipt is acknowledged of your application for appointment as a flying cadet. The commanding general directs you be informed that appropriate Air Corps units are not available at this time.

The letter went on to instruct him to reapply when "colored applicants can be given flying cadet training" (*Crisis*, March 1941, p. 87).

Snubs such as this caused the doubts and fears of young blacks to resurface continually during this period, in spite of the generally favorable overview of progress. In this instance, the end of the story is a triumph for all. Blacks were eventually integrated into all branches of the armed forces.

Yancey Williams would become a member of the United States Air Corps, but in the South, where most black Americans still resided, black men could not be assimilated into the labor force in textile mills, as it was thought that too many white women worked there. In addition to the black man/white woman conflict, the textile mills had been mechanized and blacks were deemed incompetent in the face of machinery. In contrast, the dexterity with which blacks handled the machines of the Virginia and North Carolina tobacco factories again marked them as inferior since, on this occasion, manual dexterity was seen as a trait associated with marginal intellect (Goldfield, 1990, p. 27).

As we review these decades it is important to remember that this was a period of great mechanization, mechanization that displaced black expertise in many industries. In the building trades steel was introduced, limiting the need for skilled carpenters; trucks replaced draymen; and wheelwrights and coopers were being replaced by factory machinery. Blacks were being eliminated at the low end of the labor market and barred from the professional ranks.

A continuum stretches across three and a half decades along which progress toward engineering and technological educational self-sufficiency of black Americans can be measured. One may also measure, along this continuum, the resistance to that progress. For black Americans it is a battle of peaks and troughs. The topics discussed in this chapter—teacher training, choice of institutional leaders, union eligibility, and philanthropic funding—are matters that blacks, by their strident refusal to be compliant, impacted. The degree to which this impact was felt is best seen four years beyond the scope of this research as it culminates in the *Brown* case for school desegregation.

The efforts toward educational self-sufficiency were fought on many fields. As some black schools sought to remove presidents, others in concurrent encounters sought acceptance by a different body of agencies. These agencies had the power to grant approval and acceptance to colleges and professional schools. The fight for institutional acceptance, accreditation, is a battle that once again displays the peaks and troughs that have characterized the black higher education struggle.

THE ACCREDITATION OF BLACK INSTITUTIONS

In 1890 few black Americans were familiar with the fields of engineering and technology. Forty years later, in 1930, many black Americans were aware of the field, while others, newly introduced to the idea of black participation in this area of the job market, became advocates for the lowering of exclusionary barriers. This forty-year transition is both interesting and historically noteworthy since it shows an intellectual awakening in the black community to the broad spectrum of opportunity that existed in these fields. It is also a time when struggling black institutions addressed the realities of accreditation. They were caught between the increased awareness of the black community and the financial burden that accreditation would have imposed. These pressures make this a most conspicuous time in the development of black institutions.

Accreditation for educational institutions is the seal of approval by institutional peers. Strict guidelines are established that must be met if high schools, colleges, or universities wish to be awarded the seal of an accrediting agency. Early accrediting groups were the Middle States Association of Colleges and Secondary Schools, the Southern Association of Colleges and Secondary Schools, and the New England Association of Colleges and Secondary Schools. They worked to bring a more defined meaning to the terms "high school," "college," and "university."

These three powerful associations, Middle States, New England, and Southern, came into being late in the nineteenth century and were joined in the early twentieth century by other standardizing agencies such as the College Entrance Examination Board. This group of agencies worked to establish closer ties between institutions, to standardize college admission requirements, and to improve the academic quality of college and university education.

In 1913 a fourth accrediting group, the North Central Association of Colleges and Secondary Schools, issued the first list of regionally accredited colleges and universities. This was the first time American colleges were defined by specific factual, mechanical, and uniform standards (Anderson, 1984, p. 251). Within a decade of the first list of accredited schools it became obvious that no institution could be a prominent player without the approval of these accrediting agencies. To lose the approval or to be denied the approval of one of these agencies worked to the detriment of an institution. Job opportunities, acceptance to graduate school, and the acquisition of state licensure depended heavily upon the applicant's institution.

In 1928 the Southern Association of Colleges and Secondary Schools began to rate black schools on a separate listing. Similar attempts by W.E.B. Du Bois in both 1900 and 1910 ended with a finding that Howard, Fisk, Atlanta, Morehouse, and Virginia Union were the most complete black institutions (Anderson, 1988, p. 250). In 1917, with financing from wealthy philanthropists and the Federal Bureau of Education, Jesse Jones produced a two-volume review of black colleges in which he found only Howard and Fisk to be credible institutions (Anderson, 1988, p. 251).

Most black colleges had small endowments and the institutional demands of the accrediting agencies were beyond the financial capabilities of the schools. The rating agencies demanded that colleges maintain at least six departments, or professorships, with one professor teaching full time in each department. The annual income of the college had to be sufficient to maintain professors with advanced degrees and to supply adequate library and laboratory facilities. There could be no college preparatory departments connected to the college, and there had to be an endowment of at least $200,000. In 1917 only Hampton Institute and Tuskeegee had sufficient and endowments to be considered, and both relied heavily on their preparatory programs (Anderson, 1988, pp. 249–50).

The surveys by Du Bois and later by Jones made it clear to black educators that if black colleges were going to be competitive, they could not exist apart from the power of the accrediting organizations. No matter how black the college, it would have to submit to the regulations of white agencies.

The first of the black institutions to receive a significant accreditation by a regional or national accrediting agency was Howard University, and that was for its medical school, not for its School of Engineering and Architecture. Nevertheless that institution allows us a starting point for black accreditation. At the other end of the color spectrum were schools of engineering, such as the Massachusetts Institute of Technology's, that were early recipients of accreditation.

During the period from 1890 to 1930, there was a rise in the level of professionalism in the field of engineering. Credentials were becoming important and the origin of the credential—the school from which one had graduated—was as important as the transcript itself. In April 1932, in a speech before the North Central Association of College and Secondary Schools, Walter A. Jessup, soon to be the head of this accreditation group, described the need for standardization, both in content and in length of curricula, in the accreditation of institutions and specialized programs such as engineering (Jessup, 1932, pp. 112–20).

Later in the year, William Wickenden, an early investigator of technical education, wrote an article entitled "Who and What Determines the Educational Policies of Engineering Schools?" In that article Wickenden explained the difficulties in standardizing the evolving curriculum of engineering schools. He started by describing the one-year program and the "quasi-" apprentice program that was begun in 1823 at Rensselaer, site of the first American program for engineering. This program was reorganized in 1849 and extended to three years. The poor high school preparation of entrants made it necessary to add a year of secondary school work and this was the origin of the four-year curriculum.

By 1870 several other schools had joined the list of institutions offering engineering. They were Massachusetts Institute of Technology (MIT), Columbia University, Cornell University, and the University of Michigan. For the next seventy-five years, these schools would be the accredited standard-bearers for schools of engineering (Wickenden, July 1932, pp. 228–38).

ENGINEERING OPPORTUNITIES AT HOWARD UNIVERSITY AND THE MASSACHUSETTS INSTITUTE OF TECHNOLOGY

Typical of the northern engineering schools after 1895 was MIT, a school with high academic standards, difficult entrance requirements, and a diploma that was extremely negotiable. Among black schools attempting to build programs, two schools were prominent, Howard University and Hampton Institute. By following the progress of blacks pursuing engineering degrees at Howard and MIT during the thirty-five-year period from roughly 1895 to 1930, the magnitude of the struggle that had to be waged to bring engineering education within the reach of the black community becomes clearer.

Between 1892 and 1930 MIT graduated forty engineering and technically oriented black students (see Table 2). Though their numbers may be small, the fact that this school graduated its first black as early as 1892 says something about its willingness to

Table 2
Massachusetts Institute of Technology Engineering Specializations of
Black Graduates, 1890–1930

```
Civil..................9
Mechanical..............5
Electromechanical.......2
Architecture...........2
Chemistry..............5
Electrical.............9
Chemical...............2
Mining.................1
Engineering Management..1
Not Available..........4
```

Source: Abney, 1883, p. 35.

provide access. That access at MIT led to greater exposure for many black students because the skills acquired here were often taken to the schools of the South that prepared black students. An 1892 graduate of MIT, Robinson Taylor, became the mechanical and architectural drawing instructor at Tuskeegee shortly after his graduation (Abney, 1983, p. 20). His contributions and skills placed him in a conspicuous position for many who wished to follow in his academic footsteps. He is responsible for the design and creation of the chapel and the campus library on the Tuskeegee campus.

The years of black student graduations, more than the totals, indicate something of the upsurge in interest that was awakened in the black community. The list of MIT graduates by years is shown in Table 3. From 1892 to 1921 only eleven blacks graduated, with no more than a single black in any given year. From that point forth, at least until 1929, there was always more than one black graduate, with years of five and seven. Of the forty graduates, twenty-seven graduated between 1921 and 1929, a time when many black families were not financially solvent. This meant that the only black students who would get an opportunity to attend schools of engineering, such as MIT, would be those who came from a certain economic strata or students who demonstrated

Table 3
Black Graduates of Massachusetts Institute of Technology, 1890–1930

YEAR/STUDENT	DISCIPLINE	HOMETOWN
1892		
Taylor, Robinson T.	Architecture	
1894		
Johnson, William Arthur		
1898		
Dixon, John Brown		
1899		
Dixon, Charles Sumner	Electrical	New Bedford, Ma
1900		
Smith, William Henry	Mechanical	Baltimore, Md
1903		
Smith, Daniel Arthur	Electrical	Houston, Tx
1906		
Terrell, Wendell Phillips	Mechanical	
1909		
Turner, Marie Celeste(a)	Chemistry	
1910		
Brown Jr, Dallas	Mechanical	New Bedford, Ma
1917		
Krigger, Anselmo	Civil	Cambridge, Ma
1918		
Jones, Bertram Francis	Chemistry	
1921		
Purnell, Lee Julian	Electrical	
Scott Jr, Emmett Jay	Civil	New York, N.Y.
1923		
Courtney, Roger Davis		Boston, Ma
Downing, Lewis King(b)	Eng'g Management	Roanoke, Va
Parker, Joseph Lincoln		Mount Vernon, N.Y.
1924		
Carter, John Churchel	Electrical	Washington, D.C.
Lindsey, Albert Eugene	Mining	
Smith, Victor Claude	Chemical	
Taylor, James Dennis	Architecture	Boston, Ma
1925		
Cain, Lief LittleJohn	Mechanical	Darlington, S.C.
Evan, James Carmichael	Electrical	Miami, Fla
Fassit, Andrew Jackson	Electrical	Boston, Ma
Robinson, John Bernard		
Washington, George L	Mechanical	
1926		
Circhlow, Ernest Gordon	Biology	
Cooley, Courtney Brantly	Chemistry	
Diggs, George Lyle	Electrical	Boston, Ma
Fort, Marron William	ElectroMechanical	Cambridge, Ma
Hall, Chrisper Clement	Civil	
Hope, Edward Swain (c)	Civil	Atlanta, Ga
Jewell, Paul Vernon	ElectroMechanical	Cambridge, Ma

Table 3 (continued)

YEAR/STUDENT	DISCIPLINE	HOMETOWN
1927		
Bethel, William Harold	Civil	
Bowles, George Francis	Chemical	
Edward, Arnold	Electrical	
Taylor, Westervelt A	Civil	Cambridge, Ma
1928		
Duncan, Henry Benjamin	Civil	
Solomons, Gustave Martine	Electrical	Quincy, Ma
1929		
Bethel, William Henry	Civil	Buffalo, N.Y.
Bonner, Joseph Andrew	Civil	Boston, Ma
Knox, William Jacob	Chemistry	

(a) did not receive her degree from MIT
(b) attended Howard University prior to MIT
(c) attended Morehouse College prior to MIT

Source: Wilkinson, 1977, p. 178.

exceptional ability and could win scholarship support. This is significant because at a time when public black education was being funded at low levels, the clamor for greater technical exposure increased in the black community.

These were years of extreme economic hardship for most black Americans, which meant that the ability to pay one's way became more of a hindrance to access than all of the false barriers erected by the colleges.

By looking at the hometowns of the graduates, it is obvious that at least seven were from southern cities and two had attended black colleges, Morehouse College and Howard University, before coming to MIT (Abney, 1983, pp. 16–21). The expense of attendance and the travel from southern cities to northern schools assured that the number of eligible applicants would always be small, no matter how wide the door of opportunity was opened. The "Jim Crow" travel laws and fear of physical harm also served as deterrents to northern college attendance. During the 1920s, employment opportunities for black graduates of engineering schools were severely limited.

It is astounding to note that several students overcame the hardships of both cost and distance and were among the early graduates of MIT. When the barrier of distance is removed, the statistics are equally dismal. The twenties were a time when the Boston-area school systems were noted for their tolerance and diversity. During this period, over 900 black students graduated from area school systems within a trolley's-ride distance of the MIT campus. Only nine graduated from MIT in engineering and technical studies (Abney, 1983, p. 27). They came from Quincy, Boston, and Cambridge public schools. The social climate that existed, even in the most welcoming institutions, was such that blacks obviously needed their own institutions to overcome admission, financial, and travel difficulties involved in the pursuit of their education.

By contrast, while MIT was graduating a few blacks per year, Howard University and other black institutions were laying the groundwork for a challenge to the meager number of admission slots that were distributed to blacks by the nation's engineering schools. As early as 1908 engineering courses were introduced to Howard's curriculum, and were made a full program in 1910. The early courses were in the areas of architecture, civil, electrical, and mechanical engineering. There was no separate school of engineering and as a result the courses were offered by the School of Manual Arts and Applied Sciences. It was not until 1934 that the university established a separate school of engineering and architecture (Howard University catalogue, 1988, p. 185).

Nevertheless Howard University provided an alternative to the white institutions of the day. As early as 1914, Howard graduated a student in engineering. He was Manuel A. Agosto. Between 1914, the year of the first engineering graduate, and 1930, Howard graduated forty-one engineers (Wilkinson, 1977, p. 178) (Table 5). Of that number, thirty-seven graduated between 1921 and 1930, paralleling the increase seen at MIT. This number surpasses the output of any other institution.

During the first twenty-five years of its existence. Howard's engineering program graduated fifty-nine engineers and architects

Table 4
Black Graduates of Howard University School of Engineering and Architecture, 1914–1930

YEAR/STUDENT	DISCIPLINE
1914	
Agosto, Manuel	Civil
1915	
Falu, Narcisco	Civil
Huskerson, William	Civil
1917	
Piper, Percival Robert	Electrical
1921	
Alston, Chester	Civil
Brannon, Clyde	Civil
Downing, Lewis King	Civil
Jefferson, Henry Homer	Civil
Ragsdale, Randolph David	Electrical
Thomas, William A.	Electrical
1922	
Gough, William Irving	Civil
1923	
Cheevers, Samuel R.	Civil
Ferguson, Arthur W.	Architecture
Gardner, Julius M.	Architecture
Madison, Robert J.	Civil
Taylor, James Henry	Electrical
Priestly, Alfred C.	Architecture
1926	
Brooks, Westley Herley	Architecture
Lee, Lawrence Augustus	Architecture
Logwood, Franklin Burrell	Electrical
Queen, Howard Donovan	Electrical
Welch, Ernest Rivers	Electrical
1927	
Patton, Joseph Samuel	Civil
Winder, Earl Theodore	Architecture
1928	
Batson, Thomas Everett	Electrical
Cope, Thomas C.	Electrical
1929-	
Berry, Robert Lee	Civil
Borican, Charles Henry	Electrical
Myers, Victor Talmadge	Civil
Scott, James P.	Electrical
1930	
Dabney, Walter Hampton	Civil
Mayfield, Floyd A.	Architecture
Powers, Bernard Conrad	Civil
Saunders, Thomas Henry	Civil
Welch, John Austin	Architecture

Source: Wilkinson, 1977, p. 178.

(see Table 4). This number was greater than that of any other institution in America for the production of black engineers during the early decades of this century. This new door of opportunity assured that new faces would be present in the fields of engineering and technology.

This fact seems to have passed some parties without notice since the 1939 Hurt's *College Blue Book*, the outstanding college reference of the day, did not list Howard University as a viable option—not even in the section for "coloreds." Howard University suffered from this lack of recognition in terms of engineering and architecture, but did make the publication as a medical college and a school of dentistry (Hurt, 1939, p. 327). This snub took place after twenty-five years of engineering graduations from Howard and at a time when Howard University was advertising its electrical, civil, and mechanical engineering curricula in educational journals (*Crisis*, January 1939, p. 7). Hurt's publication led the reader to believe that only two engineering schools existed in the District of Columbia: Catholic University's and George Washington University's (Hurt, 1939, p. 327).

Earlier, *The Patterson's American Educational Directory* for 1936, another of the era's authorities on colleges, listed Howard University's engineering school along with the aforementioned schools in Washington, D.C. It did, however, mention parenthetically that the school was for "Coloreds" (Patterson, 1936, p. 113).

This omission of Howard University from college information books and the unwillingness of accrediting agencies and/or engineering societies to acknowledge and respect the effort that was being made appears to be the type of racism in vogue during the thirties among the white intelligentsia. Blacks fought back. The thirties saw a new emphasis on professional and technical education and as early as 1930 Howard University boasted an engineering society of its own. Any student enrolled in the engineering or architectural curriculum was eligible for membership—a profound difference from the case of F. A. Gregory, a 1932 graduate of the Case School of Cleveland, Ohio, who was elected to Tau Beta Pi honorary engineering fraternity, a membership that was revoked when it was found that he was black (*Crisis*, August 1932, pp. 247–50).

The anger and frustration that this and similar incidents spawned is difficult to measure but meaningful if one is to understand thoroughly the barriers to black access during the thirties and forties. To appreciate fully the impact that prejudicial treatment had on black engineering aspirants who attended white schools where their future was uncertain, or those who were forced to attend black schools because these were the only doors open, one must follow them far beyond their years on campus.

THE DEVELOPMENT OF BLACK SCHOOLS OF ENGINEERING

The development of black institutions that served a professional student body was decades in the making. Both the societal constraints and the inability of blacks to underwrite the cost of such a venture made the task seem insurmountable.

In many cases the black schools that were founded between 1865 and 1917 were extended high schools that served as a hedge against black illiteracy. Often they awarded high school diplomas, normal school certificates, and college degrees. The dates of their founding show that they could not have had large student bodies prepared for the rigors of college work (Table 5). Funding was inadequate, legislative oversight was weak, and most of all, incentives for mass attendance, in both the private and the public sectors, were absent.

Schools for blacks could be divided into several categories. First there were schools provided solely by the state. These were supported by state funds and were seldom the equal of their white counterparts. Few taught strictly college courses and even fewer were adequately staffed. This was the public sector.

There were also the missionary schools, many of which had been founded in the nineteenth century shortly after the Civil War. Many of these schools proved to be the salvation of black higher education since they were administered by religious orders and not dependent upon

Table 5
Early Black American Colleges

Location	Institution	Year of Founding
Alabama		
Birmingham	Daniel Payne College	1889
Birmingham	Miles College	1902
Greenville	Lomax-Hannan College	1893
Huntsville	Oakwood College	1896
Montgomery	Alabama State College	1873
Normal	Alabama A&M College	1875
Selma	Selma University	1878
Talladega	Talladega College	1881
Tuscaloosa	Stillman College	1867
Tuskeegee	Tuskeegee Institute	1881
Arkansas		
Little Rock	Arkansas Baptist College	1884
Little Rock	Philander Smith	1877
North Little Rock	Shorter College	1886
Pine Bluff	Arkansas Agricultural, Mechanical & Normal College	1873
District of Columbia		
Washington	D.C. Teachers College	1873
Washington	Howard University	1867
Florida		
Daytona Beach	Bethune-Cookman College	1904
Jacksonville	Edward Waters College	1883
Tallahassee	Florida A&M University	1887
Georgia		
Albany	Albany State College	1903
Atlanta	Atlanta University	1865
Atlanta	Clark College	1869
Atlanta	Morehouse College	1867
Atlanta	Morris Brown College	1881
Atlanta	Spelman College	1881
Augusta	Paine College	1882
Fort Valley	Fort Valley State College	1895
Savannah	Savanna State College	1890
Kentucky		
Frankfort	Kentucky State College	1886
Louisville	Simmons College	1879
Louisiana		
Baton Rouge	Southern University	1880
Grambling	Grambling College	1901
New Orleans	Dillard University	1868

Table 5 (continued)

Location	Institution	Year of Founding
Mississippi		
Holly Springs	Mississippi Industrial College	1905
Holly Springs	Rust College	1866
Itta Bena	Mississippi Valley State College	1905
Jackson	Jackson State College	1877
Lorman	Alcorn A&M College	1871
Natchez	Natchez Junior College	1885
Prentiss	Prentiss N&I Institute	1907
Tugaloo	Tougaloo College	1869
Missouri		
Jefferson City	Lincoln University	1866
Maryland		
Baltimore	Morgan State College	1867
Baltimore	Coppin State College	1900
Bowie	Bowie State College	1867
North Carolina		
Charlotte	Johnson C. Smith University	1867
Concord	Barber-Scotia College	1867
Durham	North Carolina College	1909
Elizabeth City	Elizabeth City State College	1891
Fayetteville	Fayetteville State College	1891
Greensboro	North Carolina A&T State University	1891
Kittrell	Kittrell College	1886
Raleigh	St. Augustine College	1867
Raleigh	Shaw University	1865
Salisbury	Livingstone College	1879
Ohio		
Wilberforce	Central State University	1887
Wilberfoce	Wilberforce University	1856
Oklahoma		
Langston	Langston University	1897
South Carolina		
Columbia	Allen University	1870
Columbia	Benedict College	1870
Denmark	Voorhees College	1897
Orangeburg	Claflin College	1869
Orangeburg	South Carolina State College	1895
Rock Hill	Clinton College	1894
Rock Hill	Friendship Junior College	
Sumter	Morris College	1905

Table 5 (continued)

Location	Institution	Year of Founding
Tennessee		
Jackson	Lane College	1882
Knoxville	Knoxville College	1875
Memphis	LeMoyne-Owen College	1870
Nashville	Tennessee A&M College	1909
Nashville	Fisk University	1866
Nashville	Meharry Medical College	1876
Texas		
Austin	Houston-Tillotson College	1877
Crockett	Mary Allen College	1885
Dallas	Bishop College	1881
Hawkins	Jarvis Christian College	1912
Marshall	Wiley College	1873
Prairie View	Prairie View A&M College	1876
Tyler	Butler College	1905
Tyler	Texas College	1894
Waco	Paul Quinn College	1894
Virginia		
Hampton	Hampton Institute	1868
Lawrenceville	St Paul's College	1888
Lynchburg	Virginia Seminary College	1888
Petersburg/Norfolk	Virginia State College	1895
Richmond	Virginia Union Seminary	1865
West Virginia		
Institute	West Virginia State College	1891

Source: Jenkins, 1940, p. 131.

the state for financing. The Congregationalists founded and supported such schools as Atlanta University, Fisk University, Talladega College, Tougaloo College in Mississippi, and Hampton Institute. The Methodist Episcopal Church, the Baptist, and the AME Zion church bodies all established colleges. These private institutions served as the cornerstone of black collegiate education for nearly sixty years following the Civil War (Meier, 1968, pp. 146–47). Many of these newly formed black colleges would never receive the accreditation of an educational association, nor would they ever offer a purely collegiate curriculum. A few schools would be recognized early for their outstanding work, but even then it would only be in a very narrow category. Howard University was accredited by the Association of Medical Schools in 1912. It was the first black school to be so recognized. There would be no similar recognition by a national organization or regional accrediting agency for a black engineering school in the near future.

Between 1917 and 1930 the country experienced tremendous change. As a result of the international conflict and exposure to a new dimension of freedom, many black Americans came to see themselves as people capable of shaping their own destinies. Politically the changes meant a new militancy by returning black servicemen and a new press for both civil and voting rights (Moses, 1978, p. 247). The fear of large-scale black participation turned the country from its progressive expansionism to a cloistered repressive mode that set the stage for many types of exclusionary legislation aimed at minorities and immigrants.

In spite of this, enterprising black students found outlets for their scholarship. It is at this point that the road to black academic attainment forks, and leads both to northern schools willing to accept blacks and to racially segregated southern schools struggling to establish new programs. Both groups are worthy of praise because their efforts led to the eventual development of black schools of engineering in America.

Among the racially segregated schools in the South, the first black institution to claim a course in engineering was Tuskeegee Institute. The course was begun in 1898 and though touted as a course in electrical engineering it was a course in electricity (Pierce, 1904, p. 666). It gave students a working knowledge of the preparation, installation, repair, and maintenance of an electrical system. It also covered power station operation.

The course originated as Tuskeegee was bringing electric power to its campus. Under the direction of Charles W. Pierce the students learned by doing. They installed a fifty-kilowatt alternator, strung the lines, and even cut the timber for the poles. After three years of training they received certificates that stated that they had completed a course in engineering (Pierce, 1904, p. 673).

The course had been improperly labeled. As a course in electricity, it was fine as far as it went, but it fell far short of the sophistication and theoretical content that a true engineering course demanded. Nevertheless the course attracted students from many cities throughout this country and many from foreign lands. In 1904 Tuskeegee enrolled students in this program from Haiti,

Jamaica, Puerto Rico, Cuba, and from the states of Alabama, Georgia, Louisiana, Tennessee, Kansas, Texas, Indiana, Illinois, Montana, and the District of Columbia (Pierce, 1904, p. 666). In 1922 only one true black engineering program existed. It was located at Howard University. Howard's success was coupled with a steadily growing number of black engineering graduates from both black and white institutions. In 1922 black engineers came from Harvard University, Kansas State University, and the Case School; in 1923 from Ohio State, Cornell, and, as always, Howard University (*Crisis*, July 1922, p. 12; *Crisis*, July 1923, p. 123). In 1927 Frederick Massiah, a bright young black engineer, won the Harmon Foundation Award in the field of engineering (Downing, 1935, p. 67). The prize came as a result of his work on the Walnut Plaza Apartments in Philadelphia, a $10 million structure; and the post office in Camden, New Jersey, a $1.25 million project. Both of these undertakings were outrageously costly for the time. Massiah was not the first black to win this award but the third. He followed James A. Pearson of Dayton, Ohio, and James C. Evans of Institute, West Virginia (Downing, 1935, p. 70).

When compared with the total number of graduates for any single year or when compared with the number of engineering graduates for a single year, the number of black college students and black engineering graduates may seem insignificant. This appears so only if numbers are the sole concern. It is necessary to consider the conditions under which each of the degrees was attained. Until the 1930s, there was never a year of record in which twenty blacks graduated from the combined schools of engineering. There were, however, enough graduates to keep the belief alive that blacks could compete in the technologies. There may have been a year or two when the number of blacks approached twenty, but colleges that admitted blacks have incomplete records or claim to have been colorblind in their selection of students.

Dennis Harrison, archivist of Case University, admits that "there are no hard figures on minorities graduating from this institution for the years 1900–1930." The Sheffield School at Yale University appears to have fallen prey to the same inability to distinguish its black alumni. The Massachusetts Institute of Technology does possess a record of its black alumni during this period—a record of black participation that dates from the nineteenth century.

A critical look at the discriminatory practices of major colleges during the early twentieth century may shed some light on the extent to which white America went to deny blacks a college education. It may also explain why each small gain in graduation numbers was loudly applauded by the black community.

First, there was the extreme discrimination and often outright denial, regardless of the high school record or character references. Catholic colleges were notorious for their intolerance, and so, with few exceptions, blacks have no early twentieth century record of completion at these schools (Weinberg, 1979, p. 275). Rules and regulations that had never before been applied were formulated and enacted to bar access to black candidates (Weinberg, 1979, p. 275).

In a rare admission, Loren Miller, a 1920s black engineering student at the University of Kansas, reported that the "Dean of the Engineering School regularly calls in all colored engineering students and advises them to get out of his school" (Weinberg, 1979, p. 289).

This was the sort of climate that one might have expected on predominantly white campuses, but there were questionable situations that black students lived with on black campuses as well. Howard University, the yardstick of black educational progress, did not have a black president until 1926 (Du Bois, 1926, p. 7). This may give the reader a better idea of the restraint under which much of black education labored.

In 1927 the students at Hampton Institute, one of the schools that funneled students north to accredited schools of engineering, went on strike. Their complaint was that the recently passed Mussenberg bill, which required the separation of the races in public halls in Virginia, made the day-to-day interface with most of the faculty and the president an uneasy if not impossible task. The faculty and staff were predominantly white and in some instances openly declared membership in the Klu Klux Klan. The students were black. Dr. James E. Gregg, the Hampton's president, also hired former Klan members as faculty, including one who died on the job and was buried in full Klan regalia (*Crisis*, December 1927, p. 345). The idea that instructors often serve as role models was lost on this group of administrators, and students rebelled. For calling a strike, twenty-two members of the Student Committee were expelled.

By the mid-1920s, it was obvious that little substantive help would come from agencies outside the black community in the effort to produce black technologically oriented graduates. With this realization came a reexamination of the black community's educational stock. If there was to be a competitive school of engineering that welcomed black applicants, Howard University was the logical starting point. As an example of this institution's ability to produce the needed professionals, the years between 1923 and 1928 are particularly important. During that five-year period, a total of 586 black medical doctors were produced by American medical schools. Of that number, 475 came from the two black medical schools, Howard's and Meharry College's (*Crisis*, December 1929, p. 145). The same type of statistics can be found for nursing and dentistry. The few black schools offering the professional courses produced far more black graduates than the white schools for any comparable period. It would be the same as engineering, but it would be several years before the figures would bear this out.

THE FIGHT FOR HOWARD UNIVERSITY'S SCHOOL OF ENGINEERING: L. K. DOWNING'S CRUSADE

In addition to Hampton and Tuskeegee, two schools heavily financed by northern industrialists, there was another black postsecondary institution that survived and thrived during the difficult times of the early decades of the twentieth century. Howard University, founded in 1867, was to become the premier black institution in America. Supported by an act of Congress, the school attracted a faculty and student body that was competitive with and in many instances superior to many white postsecondary institutions (Downing, 1935, p. 63). Despite its success in producing a cadre of black professionals, Howard was seen as posing no threat to the entrenched racial separatists in Congress. They could vote for appropriations for the black school without offending their constituents "back home" and at the same time declare that they had struck a blow for equal education.

Howard University was able to eliminate all secondary school work on its campus and in 1922 form a new system in which the first two years were called the junior college and the final two years the senior college. Among the many offerings of this university were engineering and architecture. Engineering courses were introduced in 1908 and a true engineering program was begun in 1910, the first at any black postsecondary institution. By 1931 over 30 percent of all black engineering and architectural students in America attended Howard University (Downing, 1935, p. 63). By 1935 Howard was producing nearly 50 percent of all of America's black engineers, doctors, lawyers, and Ph.D.'s (Williams, 1922, pp. 157–58).

During the long struggle for fair and equal treatment by accrediting organizations and engineering societies, black colleges, despite their lack of recognition, continued to produce young men and women of substance. It became quite clear that limited admissions to schools of engineering and the inability of black institutions to enter the ranks of the "recognized" schools would allow only a fraction of the deserving students, if the 1900–1930 pattern continued, to become engineers. In the black community, the drive to recruit more blacks to schools of engineering continued. Spearheading the drive was L. K. Downing, acting dean of the College of Applied Sciences at Howard University. In a 1933 speech he reminded his audience that over $400,000,000 was scheduled to be spent by the Public Works Administration of the National Recovery Act on roads, highways, dams, water systems, and water supply projects (*Crisis*, October 1933, p. 231). He encouraged young people to enroll in Howard's architecture and engineering courses because the need in the coming decade would be overwhelming. The contributions of L. K. Downing extend beyond his encouragement of the young to become involved in the field of engineering. He is very likely the pivotal person in the development of the black schools of engineering. During the thirties, many colleges—both black and white—made the decision to abolish their costly schools of engineering. Dr. Mordecai Johnson, Howard University's president, considered closing both the architecture and the engineering schools because of the scarcity of funds. In the weeks to follow, Dean Downing evidenced both his commitment and his eloquence in defense of the schools.

Downing went to great lengths to prove that only minimal savings would be realized if Howard were to close its school of engineering. He saw the school as the basis for the development of an appreciation of technology among blacks and a means of elevating blacks to positions of parity within the world of science. While Downing's impassioned plea went to the president of the university, William P. Commady, president of the Engineering society, sent a caring response to the university trustees. Letters were also received from many other interested parties. Among them was a letter from John A. Lankford of the National Technical Association. Lankford reminded the administration of the progress that had been made during the twenty years of the school's existence. In the end, those with vision prevailed, and the administration relented. In the fall of 1985, the Howard University engineering program, then in its seventy-fifth year, celebrated A. A. Downing's work by making this episode in the school's existence the centerpiece of its journal, *Diamond Scope*. (The entire article appears in Appendix A.)

HAMPTON INSTITUTE

Hampton Institute, scarcely 100 miles south of the nation's capital, was founded in 1868 and grew to prominence in the black educational community as a producer of tradesmen. Auto mechanics, home builders, bricklayers, and carpenters had been trained there since its founding. By 1927 the Trade School of Hampton Institute offered courses in agriculture, agricultural engineering, agronomy, animal husbandry, biology, and building construction. The curriculum of the building construction course included architectural drawing, plans, working drawing, and structural design. By 1939 applied mechanics, principles of architecture, strength of materials I & II, and general physics had been added. All this was included in a four-year bachelor's program of building construction, not architecture or engineering.

In 1942, under the directorship of George W. Davis, the Armstrong-Slater Trade School of Hampton Institute proclaimed two four-year courses in Architectural Engineering and Architectural Design. For the Design curriculum, the 1942–1943 Hampton catalogue read as follows:

> It is the aim of this course to train creative architectural designers who will have the necessary preparation in engineering, professional procedure, business fundamentals, and cultural background to qualify them to meet the requirements of state examining boards for certification as architects.

In 1942 when Davis contemplated this move, Virginia was still very much a southern state.

For the engineering course the catalogue read:

> The training fits graduates to employ, organize, and direct intelligently the specialties required in modern building projects. The intensive instruction in the engineering aspects of architecture, combined with a cultural background, should prepare the graduate to be a designer of structures, field superintendent of construction, building contractor, and should prepare him to meet the educational requirements of state examining boards in structural engineering and various categories of civil service examinations.

Like Howard University, Hampton was preparing to be a factor in the coming wartime press for skilled personnel. By pointing the instruction toward the state requirement, the school was preparing its students for acceptance under the new Fair Employment Practices Commission guidelines introduced by President Roosevelt in 1941 (Morris, 1975, p. 221). Hampton presented the opportunity at a reasonable cost, $294 per year (Jenkins, 1940, p. 131). With this they hoped—unlike in the engineering societies—their graduates would be judged on the merit of their abilities and not on their racial differences.

On January 22, 1945, the first architectural engineering graduate of Hampton Institute, Cecil Gilmore Johnson, received his diploma. Johnson was probably unaware that as late as 1945, only three other black schools had ever graduated an engineer. He was followed by thirty-two additional graduates by the year 1950. Until 1948 the Hampton graduation program printed the hometowns of graduates, and from these it can be gleaned that of the thirteen young men who graduated prior to 1948, ten were from southern cities. Hampton's timely upgrade of its curriculum offerings to include engineering may have made the difference in the lives of these architects.

During the forties, when George Davis sought to bring his institution into the mainstream of technological education by opening an engineering school at Hampton, he corresponded with many respected educators. He queried established schools for information concerning their enrollments, per-student costs, and the cost of academic support for their respective programs. Downing, at Howard, was one of the first to reply (Appendix B). Some of the correspondence has been preserved by the university archivist. Among them are Davis' letter from Ovid Eschback of Northwestern University (Appendix C). It represents clear evidence of the tremendous capital outlay that was necessary to establish the type of facility he sought. The $600 annual expense allotted for the teaching of each student enrolled in engineering at Northwestern was more than double Hampton's annual tuition.

In a letter from P. V. Jewell of Tennessee A&T State College, one sees the feelings of blacks about the likelihood of governmental aid to black schools of engineering. Jewell also mentions the limited opportunities for blacks in union apprenticeships (Appendix D). Together, these letters between black and white educators bring into sharp focus the problem of the time. The high costs coupled with the unlikely circumstances of government aid made the prospect of additional black engineering schools quite bleak.

But Davis's spirits were raised when he received a letter from Ralph E. Winslow, head of the Department of Architecture at Rensselaer Polytechnic Institute of Troy, New York (Appendix E). Winslow extended an offer for Hampton to join in a 3+2 program in which Hampton, like the predominantly white Trinity College, could give its students three years of pretechnical training and then transfer them to Rensselaer for their final two years of training. This offer was a first for a black school but other predominantly white institutions, including Rutgers University and Williams College, sending their students to MIT, had participated in similar arrangements for a number of years.

In the forties Davis at Hampton, like Downing at Howard a decade earlier, was finding new challenges in areas unaccustomed to black participation. This change of direction was helped by the international conflict threatening the free world. Now America sought skilled hands in every segment of the population and that meant blacks as well as whites.

Government support went to institutions that met certain criteria as centers for teaching civilians condensed courses in architecture, engineering drawing, tool engineering, chemistry of power explosives, and management defense training. This was the Engineering Defense Training Program under the auspices of the United States Office of Education. Of the ninety-one schools designated to participate in this program, Howard University was the first black school, starting in 1941 (*Crisis*, March 1941, p. 67). It was closely followed later that same year by Hampton Institute (*Crisis*, January 1943, p. 3). Both schools graduated many minorities who went on to assume government civil service positions as junior draftsmen and many different types of technicians (*Crisis*, March 1941, p. 67). Though the positions did not display the full range of their potential, they did force whites to work side by side with blacks and to see them as productive human beings.

NORTH CAROLINA AGRICULTURAL AND TECHNICAL COLLEGE

During the years 1930–1935, the economic impact of the Depression on both blacks and whites was devastating. Jobs were scarce in all regions of the country, but in the South blacks held out little hope of deliverance. Ironically, it is here that gains would have to be made if there were going to be black engineers.

In 1930 North Carolina Agricultural and Technical College (A&T) of Greensboro, North Carolina, began preparing black engineers. It was one of two schools in that state producing engineers at the time and, needless to say, the only one open to black applicants.

North Carolina Agricultural and Technical College was founded in 1891 by an act of the state legislature as a land-grant college. Two years earlier the state had founded the North Carolina Agricultural and Mechanical College as the state institution for the preparation of white engineers but had met opposition when it applied for funding under the Morrill Act. This piece of legislation declared that states "in which a distinction of race and color are made in the admission of students could qualify for federal aid only upon providing a proportionate share of such funds for the training of Negro youth."

This stipulation, rather than the wish to educate young blacks, lies at the base of the inauguration of the effort and final acceptance of the idea of the college. The college was begun hastily and for the first two years was sited on the campus of Shaw University in Raleigh, North Carolina. Two years later it was moved to Greensboro and assumed its present name in 1915.

North Carolina A&T was accredited by the State Department of Public Instruction in 1927, making it possible for graduates to receive a teaching certificate and to qualify for further study. But there were no plans to start an engineering department at the school. Numerous requests for funding were met with usual denials. Among the standard denials that were often used were: there are no funds for the equipment or teaching personnel; there is too much opposition by organized labor to the inclusion of such courses in publicly funded black institutions; to invest in black schools of engineering would be a waste of resources since there are very few positions in the field that would be available to blacks.

With heavy investments in technical courses, math, laboratory sciences, and associated subjects, the basic necessities for the establishment of an engineering curriculum were present with or without additional state funding. With this, the school put into place a program and began to graduate engineers in 1939. This date is significant since its accreditation by the Association of Collegiate Schools of Architecture would not come for more than a decade.

North Carolina A&T, like Howard University's School of Engineering, was a nonschool as far as the college directories were concerned. During the thirties and well into the forties, no black school of engineering south of Washington, D.C., was listed.

It is easy to regard this institution as only providing increased access for blacks and to ignore the other advantages that it brought. Often lost is the financial and geographical leverage that this school offered its interested students. First, as late as 1939, the tuition was decidedly lower than those of surrounding schools. Howard's was a moderate $150 per year while A&T boasted a tuition rate of only $37 per year (Hurt, 1939, p. 327). Yet this rate of tuition proved exorbitant at times, since the two schools appealed to entirely different clientele. Howard drew was from a more urban, more economically able strata of black society while the North Carolina school drew from a poorer, more rural population.

Add to this the fact that the North Carolina school was in the Deep South and the access problem, in terms of distance traveled, was lessened. This meant that in addition to all other advantages, black children could direct their talents toward a goal with greater assurance that their hopes and aspirations would reach fruition. This school also provided a wholesome on-campus social life, a rare phenomenon for any black engineering student. There is little wonder that, to this day, this school continues to produce a significant percentage of all black engineers.

Howard University, North Carolina Agricultural and Technical College, and Hampton Institute, all southern schools, were the first black schools to produce engineers. Each school can boast of its unique contributions: Howard, that its program predates 50 percent of all engineering programs in America and that its graduates account for a significant percentage of all black engineers in America and throughout the world.

Hampton can boast of the many black architects and architectural firms in which its graduates are involved and that its graduates are part of the effort to design and build a new South. The North Carolina school, proud of its historical contributions, can now be viewed as the school that produces the most black engineers.

Today much of the hardship that accompanied these advances is forgotten or, like many other such facts, has been submerged. Fortunately, there are those who can recount their struggles to young black students in an effort to inspire those students to meet today's challenges and, as they did, overcome them. Many such stories can be found and in the following chapter, three will be presented. Two were chosen because of the alma maters of the subjects, Hampton and North Carolina Agricultural and Technical College; the third because his feats of excellence are a five-decade success story, the kind most black students may never hear.

Chapter 4

Three Black Engineers

This chapter is devoted to three men who overcame institutional obstacles to become contributing members of the engineering and technological fields. The story of each is an interesting commentary on the opportunities that existed during the first half of the twentieth century for blacks who wished to be a part of the technological world. If taken separately, they show the perseverance of three individuals who were determined to find a contributing role in this society. But when we consider that these must have been men of exceptional perseverance, we must also wonder about the number of would-be contributors who refused to be humiliated by society's denials.

The three men are Gordon Grady, Archie Alexander, and Henry Livas. Grady's research played a role in the stabilization of heat in the first moon orbiter. Alexander was the first nationally acclaimed black civil engineer to win high praise for his work throughout the nation. Livas established the first black architectural firm in the southern United States, a firm that still exists.

These stories are atypical because they tell of black engineers who were able to overcome the many barriers of their society. They are atypical because they tell of black success. More often than not, blacks wishing to participate in the technologies were dissuaded.

GORDON GRADY, ENGINEER

Gordon Grady is important because he typifies many blacks who overcame the denials of a segregated society. His story is the story of an individual assuming an ever-expanding role throughout his professional career. In a long and detailed conversation with me, Mr. Grady relived the days immediately following his graduation from college, presenting them in the light of the new racial coexistence today. Grady was a 1934 public school product of West Southern Pines High School, North Carolina. The fact that he had attended school in North Carolina meant that he knew of the options at North Carolina Agricultural and Technical College, and that he could stay within his home state to attend college. This, plus the very low tuition, made the North Carolina school his first and only choice. Grady arrived at the school with insufficient funds but was granted a scholarship that required he work as kitchen help throughout his school career.

Gordon Grady graduated in 1940 with a Bachelor of Science degree in electrical engineering. He was among the first students to graduate from this school with such a degree; A&T, as it is affectionately called, was an almost forgotten engineering school in 1940. As a hedge against the realities of the workplace, he took the necessary courses for a North Carolina teaching certificate.

The engineering positions that may have been available to white graduates of other schools were not open, in many cases, to graduates of black institutions, especially in the South. As a result, Gordon Grady went home to Southern Pines to teach math, physics, and chemistry in his former high school.

After three years in the public school system of his hometown, Grady took advantage of the war and the need for skilled workmen to seek other employment. His next job took him to Norfolk, Virginia, to the Norfolk Navy Yard.

For three years Gordon Grady worked at the Norfolk installation as a third-class electrician with little hope of advancement, in spite of his preparation. If there was to be any solace gathered from this three-year sojourn, it was that his pay rose from $85 per month as a North Carolina schoolteacher to $72 per week as a Navy Yard electrician. Concurrently he taught marine electricity to many of the trainees and helpers from the Navy Yard in a vocational school program in Norfolk.

During the forties Grady held several jobs, all related to his area of expertise, but none that gave him the title of engineer with the associated responsibilities. He worked at Radio Corporation of America (RCA) in Camden, New Jersey, as a technician; then at ITE Circuit Breaker Company as a technician. Each meant an increase in pay, but never an increase in the scope of responsibility. He then worked for several small companies that needed an engineer in order to become eligible for certain government contracts. Most of these assignments were those of a high-grade technician but the experience and exposure greatly improved his practical engineering knowledge. The assignments covered areas in electrical, mechanical, and chemical engineering.

In 1951, in response to a classified ad announcing openings for engineers, Grady applied for an opening at the Honeywell plant in Philadelphia. In his telephone conversation with the personnel manager he assumed the job would be his since his experience dovetailed with the job requirements. However, when he arrived for the interview there were other job applicants seated in the waiting room. Soon the personnel manager came out to page Mr. Gordon Grady, engineering applicant. As he eyed the roomful of men it became increasingly obvious that the applicant he sought was the lone black man in the group. In the interview that followed, Grady was told that a young man had come in "just a moment ago" with qualifications that exceeded his and that that young man—not Grady—would be given the job.

The personnel office was glass-fronted, allowing a person passing in the hall to look into the office. As Grady left this appointment he looked back with disgust at the personnel manager, and as he did so, he saw his résumé thrown into the trash can. This was 1951, this man had an engineering degree, this was Philadelphia. While at RCA, Grady was fortunate to find a manager who believed he was qualified to be hired as an engineer. He arranged interviews for Grady in various departments and fortunately one manager in test engineering accepted him for an engineering position. Unfortunately, he was denied the position because the remaining engineers threatened to walk out if he was hired into their area.

These two episodes point out more clearly than do statistics the difficulties that blacks faced seeking entry into this field. It may also help to explain the high level of frustration common among black college-trained people during this time period. That feeling of complete frustration and impotence remains a great part of the black legacy to this day.

Fourteen years would pass after his graduation from an engineering program before Gordon Grady would be hired as an engineer. In 1954 he was hired as an electronic engineer at the United States Naval Material Center in Philadelphia. By then he was thirty-eight years old, married, and terribly disillusioned by the treatment he had received at the hands of his countrymen. From 1954 to 1962, Grady turned all of his collected abilities toward proving that as a black engineer his contributions could and should be as significant and as valued as any employee's at this naval installation.

As a result of his dogged determination, he rose through the ranks from electronic engineer in 1954 to electronic scientist and then in 1959 to supervisor and research engineer. This job and the manner in which he was to target his talents did more to restore his self-respect and lost hope than any of the many events that were to follow.

In 1955, a year after the *Brown v. Board of Education* case, Gordon Grady, once a student at the prestigious Moore Graduate School of Engineering, reentered the University of Pennsylvania as a graduate student, again in the engineering department. Three years later he graduated with a master's degree in electrical engineering. His success at the University of Pennsylvania came at the same time as his success at the Naval Air Material Center. By 1958, Grady, with little help from others, rebuilt his professional life.

Looking only at his entry into the Moore School of Engineering at the University of Pennsylvania it seems reasonable to ask, "On what basis was he allowed to enter such a prestigious school?" To answer this, you must know the man.

In 1960, had Grady not accepted a position with the General Electric Company, his professional life would have been a success, but his involvement with the Institute of Environmental Science demonstrates the overall commitment with which Grady approached his profession. The Institute is a professional society of engineers, scientists, and educators dedicated to the researching, simulating, testing, and teaching of the environments of the earth and space, for the betterment of mankind and the advancement of industry, education, and science. There were twenty-six chapters throughout the country when Grady joined in 1962 while working in King of Prussia, Pennsylvania.

From 1962 to 1969, Grady served with distinction as a member of the mid-Atlantic chapter of this organization. He received commendations from the national office in 1965–1966, the same year that his status rose from member to senior member, a year prior to his appointment to fill an unexpired term as chapter director.

The following year he was voted in by the membership and served a full term. Undoubtedly this sounds much like the story of any interested professional working with his peers, but hidden is the tremendous burden that Grady carried as one of fewer than ten black members of this organization that numbered more than 1600.

When he represented his chapter at the 1966–1967 annual technical meeting in St. Louis as a panel member, he saw no other black participant. It is easy to forget that this was 1967 and black engineers less certain of their identities and self-worth were having their own problems adjusting to the overwhelmingly white workplace. Grady was beyond that. When he transferred to the Boston chapter in 1970, he became the local publicity chairperson for the chapter. In 1971, he became the national publicity chairman; in 1973 he was voted vice president of the Boston chapter; and in 1974 he received two honors: he was voted the president of the Boston chapter of the Institute of Environmental Sciences, as well as a national director.

After 1974, he worked as a national officer of the organization, first as the vice president of Region I and then as vice president for Membership. In 1980 his senior membership status was that of "Fellow." In 1982, two years before his retirement, his status was changed to "Retired Fellow" with life membership. Surely, if any man made a mockery of the system that had deprived both him and other blacks from reaching their full potentials, Gordon Grady is such a man.

In situations like this the question invariably arises, "What might he have accomplished had there been no barriers?" That question is best answered by observing those who have had the opportunities without the restrictions. That blacks have not made the volume of contributions their racial presence in this society might suggest, says more about the world in which they labored than it does about their abilities in the fields of technology. Gordon Grady is now at peace with his accomplishments and his life work, but there are those who graduated a year or two after him, from colleges no longer remembered, who never reached Philadelphia or Lynn, Massachusetts. For them and for those who were discouraged long before they started, the country continues to pay a price.

ARCHIE ALEXANDER, ALEXANDER THE GREAT

Archie Alexander is important to all students of engineering. His work changed the face of the nation's capital, his accomplishments changed the nation's view of black technological contributions, and his memory can serve to inspire generations of engineers to come.

Much of Alexander's work came at a time when blacks needed a true contributor to lend meaning to their efforts. And although through the 1940s black engineering hopefuls were provided with new opportunities, it was Alexander who made a nation examine its conscience and its policies.

There are many stories that must be told to convey the true mood of the time and the story of Archie Alexander is certainly one of those. It is particularly important if one is to examine both the promise and the frustration of this decade. The information for the Archie Alexander story comes from an article in the *Palimpsest*, the journal of the Iowa State Historical Department/Office of the State Historical Society, 1985.

In the annals of black engineering, there is one little-known and seldom-told story that illustrates the capacity and commitment of one man who overcame tremendous odds to excel in his field. Born in Ottumwa, Iowa, Archie Alphonso Alexander grew to manhood in a state where only a handful of black citizens resided. He attended the schools in his home state and entered the University of Iowa in 1908. "Alexander the Great," as he was known by football fans of that era, graduated in 1912 after spending his tenure as the lone black in the university's school of engineering.

He entered a world in which his chances of success were minimal. He had been warned by the dean of the engineering school that "a Negro could not hope to succeed as an engineer." Upon his graduation, the city of Des Moines turned down his application for employment, and he was forced to accept a twenty-five cent per hour laborer's job with the Marsh Engineering Company of Des Moines. Two years later he left Marsh to establish his own company. He was then making $70 per week.

While working at Marsh, he met a white engineer named George F. Higbee and in 1917 they formed a partnership. He changed the name of his firm from A. A. Alexander to Alexander and Higbee. The partnership endured and prospered until Higbee's death in 1925. For the next four years, Alexander continued the business alone. It was during this period that he received several large contracts for construction projects from his alma mater. They included the university's new heating plant, built in 1924; its new power plant, built in 1926; and the remarkable Under-the-Iowa-River tunnel system, built in 1928.

In 1929, Maurice A. Repass, another white engineer and former classmate, joined the firm and once again the firm was renamed, this time Alexander and Repass. Prior to coming to the firm, Repass had served as an instructor in the Department of Hydraulics and

Mechanics at the University of Iowa. The firm continued to prosper and by 1930 the company had offices in Des Moines and Washington, D.C.

Alexander was a heavy contributor to the efforts of the Republican party and as a result was "well connected" in terms of political muscle when bidding for statewide or federal contracts. Over the years, the firm bid on and won contracts in all forty-eight states. By 1950 it had over three hundred major projects to its credit, many of them completed during the forties. Perhaps the most prominent were those completed in the nation's capital: the Tidal Basin bridge and seawall; the K Street elevated highway and underpass from Key Bridge to 27th Street; and the Whitehurst Freeway along the Potomac River, which carried the traffic around Georgetown.

But custom was not to be forgotten and Washington, D.C. was not about to abandon its long-held racist attitudes simply because a black contractor was in town. The city demanded that the toilet facilities be segregated. In an effort to evade the rule, Alexander labeled the facilities skilled and nonskilled, rather than black and white. In the end it had the same effect since in his crew of 200 workmen, only five of the skilled workers were black. It is ironic that Alexander, one of the nation's leading structural engineers, could not hire skilled black workmen in the nation's capital. Union restrictions and the relentless union stand against black membership during the forties meant that, regardless of their persuasion, contractors were forced to adhere to the union hiring policy.

At age 64, a prominent Republican for many years, Alexander was appointed governor of the Virgin Islands, only the second black to hold such a position. Alexander's story is a rare one but one that far too often is submerged. His success could have served as an inspiration for decades of black engineering hopefuls but few ever knew of his immense accomplishments. On January 4, 1958, Alexander died, leaving portions of his wealth to his alma mater, the University of Iowa; Tuskeegee Institute; and Howard University for engineering scholarships.

Thus passed Archie Alphonso Alexander of Ottumwa and Des Moines, a man who, in not heeding the advice of his college President, made the most of his education (Wynes, 1958, pp. 79–86).

HENRY L. LIVAS

Another black architect who could serve as a role model for any young person interested in one of the technologies is Henry L. Livas. Henry Livas was born at the time when the outlook for black Americans interested in the technologies was extremely bleak. In spite of those limited opportunities, Henry Livas persevered to become a force in the technologies of the day. He is included because he demonstrates the unwillingness of many blacks to succumb to the racist climate of pre-1950 America.

Livas was educated in the public schools of Paris, Kentucky. In 1931 Livas left his hometown to attend Hampton Institute. Henry Livas graduated from Hampton in 1935 from a building construction curriculum. That curriculum included such classes as principles of architecture, strength of materials, architectural drawing, plans and working drawings, structural design, applied mechanics, and physics. Hampton did not begin its engineering sequence until 1942, but many of the courses were in place during the years of Livas' attendance.

Shortly after graduation Livas applied, sight unseen, for a position with the Ford Motor Company of Detroit, Michigan. His résumé had won him the job, but upon his arrival he was refused the position. Livas was black; the position was intended for a white applicant.

Undaunted, Livas went back to Virginia to find work as a draftsman with the Union Realty & Insurance Company and the Michael Baker Company, where he worked until 1942. In 1942 he enrolled at Wayne State University but after one semester Livas was unable to continue. In 1945 he was awarded a graduate stipend scholarship at Pennsylvania State University. He graduated in 1945 with a master's degree in architectural engineering.

Equipped with the necessary credentials, Henry Livas now began a two-pronged career as both a commercial architect and a teacher. As a commercial architect Henry Livas became the first black licensed architect in the state of Virginia, founding in 1948 the firm of Livas and Associates. It was likewise the first black architectural firm in that state. The firm was headquartered in Hampton, Virginia, with additional offices in Norfolk. Throughout his career Livas was noted for the encouragement and guidance he gave to his students. As a result, all of the "associates" in his firm were his former students.

As a teacher of young aspirants he served as the director of mechanical arts at Arkansas Agricultural, Mechanical, and Normal College and then returned to his alma mater, Hampton, as a professor of architecture and architectural engineering. Livas taught and worked as an architect for more than thirty years. He was licensed in at least six states and the District of Columbia. He planned many churches and office buildings throughout Virginia and North Carolina. He was also instrumental in revamping the face of the Hampton campus. Those building designs for which he is best remembered are the Hampton Roads Boys Club of Newport News, Virginia; the Bay Shore Auditorium, Bay Shore Beach, Virginia; the Tyne Street Baptist Church, Suffolk, Virginia; Faculty Housing at Langston University; and Community Hospital, in Suffolk, Virginia.

He was a member of the American Institute of Architects, of which he had been national president and editor of its journal, and a member of the American Society of Engineering Education. He was a member of the association of Collegiate Schools of Architecture; Sigma Lambda Chi, an honorary building construction fraternity; the Quarter Century Club of Hampton Institute; and the NASA-ASSEE System Design Team Fellowships.

Henry Livas died on June 10, 1979, but his reputation as a designer is continued by the firm, The Livas Design Group. The firm continues to influence the face of the Hampton campus. Included in the management are at least three of his former students: William Milligan, Albert Walker, and the present head of

Hampton's School of Architecture, John Spencer. Livas' son has continued the family technical expertise. He too is an engineer. These stories of black engineering successes are included because these men formed the thread of hope that other black engineering hopefuls grasped between 1930 and 1950. Each, at some time in his career, suffered tremendous defeats because of racial bigotry; each knew severe job discrimination; and each must have realized very early in his career that the dream he held was a solitary dream, not one held by many. In each instance there are powerful lessons that can be learned.

The first is excellence. Here are three men who strove for excellence in their craft. Even in the midst of America's twentieth-century racial climate they excelled. Perseverance, tenacity, belief in oneself, and in the end, the willingness to share their knowledge with those who followed, are all powerful lessons to be gleaned from the lives of Grady, Livas, and Alexander. Equally important is the fact that these three men form a continuous chain of contributions from 1906 to the present and many of those contributions remain as significant parts of America's whole.

There are also the lessons of confidence that one teaches when he enters a new region. Each of these men compiled a great list of firsts for people of color. These are all lessons that young people, both black and white, must receive if they are to make similar contributions.

Chapter 5

The Era of the *Brown* Decision and Sputnik

During the late 1940s and the early 1950s, several items of interest surfaced concerning black collegiate attendance. First, black collegiate attendance was up by 54 percent since 1940 (McAdam, 1971, p. 102). There was also a 250 percent upsurge in the amount of philanthropic support for black postsecondary institutions. The increased attendance was due in part to the returning servicemen and the renewed interest in education that was spawned by the G.I. Bill.

The philanthropy was due in part to the aftermath of the 1938 Gaines decision that warned southern and border states that an assault on "white only" collegiate institutions was imminent if they did not provide equal facilities for blacks. The same fear caused states to increase their appropriations to black institutions.

Amid this flurry of activity at midcentury, a small but significant first occurred in Washington, D.C. In 1947 Western Electric became the first national firm to include a black engineering school as part of its annual recruiting function. The school was Howard University and at the time its engineering school was over thirty years old (Purcell, 1971, p. 20).

As 1950 approached there were nearly 63,000 blacks attending America's colleges, more black college students than at any other period in the nation's history. Over 97 percent of them were enrolled at historically black colleges and universities (*Crisis*,

August 1950, p. 488). Black institutions were better financed than at any time in our history. Much of the increased support was to stave off the impending showdown of separate educational facilities. As the support for black schools increased, the level of funding for out-of-state graduate and professional education fell sharply. But on the campuses throughout the South, the level of unrest was greater than at any previous time.

The decade of the fifties exposed many of the inequities that blacks had endured since Emancipation. Tuskegee Institute's Black Data Center reported that 1952 was the first year since 1881 in which the lynching of a black person was not reported (Sloan, 1971, p. 35). It was to be a time of new beginnings, a decade of raised hopes, a decade of rapid expansion of opportunities for young blacks interested in engineering and technology.

In education, the fifties was most notably the decade of the 1954 *Brown v. Board of Education* decision. This court case was the culmination of fifty years of continuous litigation by black Americans for parity in access to public education. The *"Brown* Case," as it is often called, was a compilation of six school discrimination cases from six widely scattered areas of the nation. The finding in this case declared that the long-accepted practice of separate but equal public education was unconstitutional.

The ramifications of this ruling were many. Not only was the message sent to public school districts that discrimination in educational access was unconstitutional, but higher education also realized that it would be the target of the next assault unless it began to address this question.

But the court victory would not immediately change the long-entrenched values of the South. In 1955 the Georgia Education Board declared that anyone teaching a "mixed" class would be banned from teaching for life in that state (Sloan, 1971, p. 40). On the collegiate level black student protest, beginning in the mid-1950s, made known the degree of unrest that black Americans felt. Students from traditional black colleges in the South led the fight for parity in both public accommodation and higher education. Student strikes on formerly all-white campuses, much like student sit-ins protesting discrimination in public accommodations, became regular occurrences. It was useless for blacks to look to Washington, D.C., for assistance since President Dwight D. Eisenhower was never a vocal supporter of the *Brown* decision. Throughout his tenure as president he never endorsed the Supreme Court's finding. For all Americans, but with special attention to black children living in the South, Eisenhower's presidency did little to move the nation toward parity in education (Ambrose, 1984, p. 337). In some states the legislative process moved educational institutions toward integrated student bodies. In 1964–65, the New York state legislature passed laws and appropriated funds to allow more minorities to attend public colleges and universities (Weinberg, 1977, p. 329). The College Discovery and SEEK programs were inaugurated to ensure that black and Puerto Rican students in New York City could matriculate at public institutions.

However, the push for school integration was not among the high-priority items for the national administration. President Eisenhower had long relied on southern votes to carry his political program and, in many ways, turned a blind eye to the poor record of educational parity and public accommodation that persisted in the South in spite of the *Brown* decision and the passage of the Civil Rights Act of 1957.

It was not until the nation suffered the scientific embarrassment of Sputnik that real attention was paid to the disparities of public education. Sputnik was the Russian intercontinental ballistic missile (ICBM), the first of its kind. The launching of this ICBM did more to spur American interest in educational reform as a means of aiding American technology than did any of the previous pleas of American scientists and engineers for assistance and funding. Sputnik caused the American military community and the academic community to begin looking for solutions to the gap that Sputnik had exposed in our domestic technology. In certain communities it was obvious that there were populations of Americans that had been written off as contributors. At the time of the launching of Sputnik, the American engineering community numbered approximately 500,000. Women accounted for less than 1 percent; blacks accounted for less than 1 percent.

This feat also showed America that sophisticated technology could give a military edge to our adversaries. In an effort to bridge the technology gap, Eisenhower allocated monies for math and science education, a preparatory step toward the production of much-needed engineering and technologically trained students (Ambrose, 1985, p. 649).

Overall, the administration's overtures to education were slight, but it was Eisenhower who instituted the first nationally funded financial aid program as part of the National Defense Education Act. In 1957 Eisenhower reluctantly allocated funds to underwrite 10,000 scholarships for the neediest students (Ambrose, 1984, p. 459). For poor Americans this would mean that poverty would no longer stand as a barrier to collegiate training, but whether it would mean greater access for underrepresented groups in previously white fields, no one could say in the 1950s.

Chapter 6

The Sixties

In 1960 the *Southern School News* reported that despite the *Brown* case, 94 percent of all black students were still attending racially segregated schools. Nevertheless, by 1962 2000 black students were enrolled in formerly all-white colleges of the South (Purcell, 1971, p. 43).

As early as 1960 it was obvious that black enrollment at the nation's engineering schools would spiral upward. But if the *Brown* case had exposed anything it had exposed the poor primary and secondary education available in the black communities. Now, even with the barriers lowered, the task of successfully completing the difficult demands of the engineering curriculum became a problem. Engineering would remain outside of the choices made by most black American collegians not only because of poor secondary school preparation, but also because of the lack of opportunity in the workplace for black engineers. In fact, more than half the degrees granted to black graduates in the 1962–1963 school year were in education, a true reflection of the existing 1960s job opportunities for blacks (Wilcox, 1971, p. 176).

As far north as Boston the systematic destruction of hope through education was being chronicled by Jonathan Kozol in his prize-winning book, *Death at an Early Age*. This book was called the most powerful and shocking book of 1967. It told the story of the post-*Brown* Boston public school system in which many black American children were trapped. Kozol, in 1968, maintained that school systems such as this systematically destroyed children's hearts and minds. If the nation was going to produce a cadre of black engineers, the likelihood of them coming from school systems such as this was minimal.

At the time that President John F. Kennedy made his brave statement about sending a man to the moon it was obvious to many that a reservoir of talent existed that would continue to lie fallow unless strident reforms were enacted. In America until 1960, engineering was a white, male enclave. It had been so since its inception. But demographic evidence forced the industrialists to look to other populations for their ever-growing needs. This meant educational reform, financial aid for deserving students too poor to pay their way, outreach to all segments of the minority and female communities, and affirmative action in hiring and placement of successful candidates. If successful, a plan such as this could produce more technically trained black people than ever before. It would also mean that many of the old stereotypes and preconceptions would have to be buried if the necessary workers were to be trained.

If relief for blacks wishing to enter this industry were to come, it would have to occur as a result of government intervention. It would require massive infusions of funds and a new assessment of the potential of those who were traditionally overlooked and forgotten. In America, this meant black people. In 1960 President Kennedy declared that the nation would put a man on the moon within the decade. This, while the nation's math and science scores were falling and a large segment of the school-age population attended substandard institutions.

In the early sixties, blacks wishing to become engineers had few examples of success in the industries that relied heavily on engineering expertise. As an example, in the late sixties and early seventies most blacks in the electrical industry held blue-collar jobs. Jobs requiring an engineering or technical background represented 36 percent of that industry's positions; positions that blacks seldom occupied. Another 12 percent of the electrical industry's jobs were those of unionized craftsmen, a field from which blacks had traditionally been barred (Purcell, 1971, p. 37). In response to the small applicant pool of blacks for engineering schools, several traditionally white colleges banded together in an attempt to:

a. strengthen black institutions,
b. identify and support promising black candidates for college admission, and
c. strengthen the precollege background of potentially able students.

Those schools were Oberlin, Yale, Harvard, Tufts, Brown, Dartmouth, Cornell, the University of Wisconsin, Carnegie Tech, Reed, and the University of Michigan (Wilcox, 1971, p 178). In the past these schools had extended "two plus two" program offers to schools with student bodies similar to their own. Now they began to widen their net to include black schools as well. Some of the affiliations were Brown with Tougaloo College of Tougaloo, Mississippi; Cornell with Hampton Institute of Virginia; the University of Michigan with Tuskeegee; and the University of Wisconsin with Texas Southern, North Carolina A&T, and North Carolina College (Wilcox, 1971, p. 178). Each of the sponsoring schools had a school of engineering. In each case the arrangement made it possible for blacks to attend engineering schools at costs that were not prohibitive and opened the possibilities for opportunities for graduate education.

Programs such as these provided sorely needed opportunities for students and faculty. Usually there was a component that provided for faculty exchange and consultation, seminars centered around curriculum development, advisory conferences on administrative procedures, and joint research projects (Wilcox, 1971, p. 178). The black colleges in these consortia learned fast and learned well.

For black schools, the opportunity to upgrade procedures and improve curricula and methodology was important since as late as 1965 black schools educated the overwhelming majority of black collegians. As a result of these and other affiliations and the determination to produce quality graduates, the schools included in these consortia were destined to become the schools that produced most of the black engineers in America.

The black students that were accepted at these institutions did not rest on their laurels; rather, they agitated for broader acceptance of black applicants. Among the demands that black students made of the host campuses was that money be appropriated for remediation and academic assistance. They also insisted on quotas to assure themselves that the customary exclusion and discrimination would not bar future applicants.

Chapter 7

The Seventies

Throughout the 1970s the verbal and math SAT scores of college-bound high school seniors dropped. Male verbal scores dropped thirty-one points while those of females dropped forty-one points. In math, a similar downward move was taking place; male scores in math dropped eighteen points while female scores dropped twenty-two points (NSF, 1982, p. 124).

By the decade of the seventies, it was obvious that serious defects were to be found in the testing system that qualified students for college science and math curricula. Blacks protested that the SAT tests that traditionally served as the license for entry into these fields were biased in favor of whites, more specifically, middle-class whites. Black SAT scores were drastically lower than white scores. In 1976–1977 the verbal scores of black college-bound high school seniors were 120 points lower than whites, while the math scores showed a difference of 135 points.

To add to the testing controversy, female verbal scores were lower eight of the ten years during the 1970s while female math scores were lower every year (NSF, 1978, p. 124). Now the protests of blacks who said the test was unfair was joined by women who declared there was a conspiracy to dissuade women from achieving excellence in math and the sciences. The wide disparities of scores resulting from the SAT testing program was first thought to indicate that blacks and women were less suited for the tasks of the engineering field and that therefore their representation in these fields was justifiably low.

The 1978–1979 Graduate Record Examination (GRE) scores for students wishing to pursue engineering seemed to duplicate the differences in testing experienced by the SAT-takers of a year earlier. Whites scored higher than blacks or Asians; men scored higher than women. There was no real change in outcome even after four years of exposure to similar training. At this point the protests mounted and alterations were begun on the testing instrument. Since that time the scores of black applicants have risen slowly though they are not yet the equivalent of white applicants' scores. The College Board has continued to pursue this problem and has established the Equity 2000 program. This program is based on research that shows that low-income blacks who master algebra and geometry attend and graduate from college at almost the same rate as higher-income white students (Collison, 1991, p. A27). The research shows that gatekeeper secondary school courses include algebra and geometry. Students who are well versed in these subjects go on to college. In fact, the research shows that 80 percent of black students who take these courses and 83 percent of white students who take those courses go on to college, virtually eliminating the racial gap. The problem seems to lie somewhere in the counseling and directing of black middle school and high school students. It is here that the College Board hopes to target its assistance.

There was also a noticeable drop in the dropout rate for black teenagers during the seventies and well into the eighties. In 1967 the black dropout rate was nearly twice that of whites. If we look at males as an isolated group, the black dropout rate was more than twice that of whites in 1967. By 1989 the rates were nearly identical (Table 6). Much of that improvement came as a result of the national campaigns aimed at black youth by government, educational, and religious groups.

Table 6
Percentage of High School Dropouts Among Persons 16 to 24 Years Old,
by Sex, Race, and Ethnicity: October 1967 to October 1989

Year	All Races	White	Black	Men White	Men Black	Women White	Women Black
1967	17.0	15.4	28.6	14.7	30.6	16.1	26.9
1968	16.2	14.7	27.4	14.4	27.1	15.0	27.8
1969	15.2	13.6	26.7	12.6	26.9	14.6	26.7
1970	15.0	13.2	27.9	12.2	29.4	14.1	26.6
1971	14.7	13.4	23.7	12.6	25.5	14.2	22.1
1972	14.6	13.7	21.5	13.1	22.3	14.2	20.8
1973	14.1	12.9	22.3	12.5	21.6	13.3	22.9
1974	14.3	13.2	21.3	13.4	20.1	13.1	22.3
1975	13.9	12.6	22.8	12.0	22.8	13.2	22.8
1976	14.1	13.3	20.4	13.2	21.2	13.3	19.7
1977	14.1	13.4	19.7	13.9	19.5	12.8	20.0
1978	14.2	13.4	20.2	13.6	22.5	13.2	18.2
1979	14.6	13.6	21.2	14.0	22.5	13.1	20.0
1980	14.1	13.3	19.3	14.2	21.1	12.3	17.9
1981	13.9	13.8	18.5	14.5	20.0	13.2	17.2
1982	13.9	13.1	18.4	13.6	21.1	12.7	16.0
1983	13.7	12.9	18.1	14.1	19.8	11.7	16.5
1984	13.1	12.7	15.6	13.5	16.7	11.8	14.5
1985	12.6	12.2	15.7	13.0	16.1	11.3	15.3
1986	12.1	11.9	13.7	12.8	14.4	11.1	13.0
1987	12.7	12.5	14.5	13.0	15.7	12.0	13.5
1988	12.9	12.7	14.9	13.5	15.4	11.9	14.4
1989	12.6	12.4	13.8	13.4	14.9	11.4	12.9

Source: *Digest of Educational Statistics*, 1990

The mid-seventies saw a rise in black participation in engineering-related fields. Their numbers rose to approximately 40,000, still only 1.5 percent of the nation's total engineering workforce. This total was eight times as great as the 1950 total for engineering-related fields, yet the 1989 National Science Foundation publication, *Science Indicators 1978*, emphasized the low level of black participation after reviewing the level of enrollment at various engineering schools (NSF, 1979, p. 138). Somehow the decision of black people, when not in accord with that of the national thrust, is always seen as faulty or incorrect. At the time that these statements were made, black engineers had a higher unemployment rate and a lower wage scale than their white counterparts (NSF, 1979, p. 136). When blacks reached college level the likelihood of finding black role models was slight. In educational institutions whites were far more likely to be tenured than the infrequent black faculty member and more likely to hold the rank of full professor, (NSF, 1982, p. 14).

Invariably, the journals of the 1970s discussed the absence of blacks in engineering as a deficiency in the ability of blacks, the poor preparation of blacks, or a combination of the two. The history of the profession and those institutions that prepare our engineers is rarely the topic of discussion. The blatant racism that has existed well into the nineties has always been a deterrent to black entry. Prior to 1950, the profession was able to erect an almost impenetrable curtain that held blacks at bay.

The long struggle for educational parity in the nation's public schools may well point to a truer cause for the scant black presence. The complexities of the engineering curriculum cannot be mastered by students whose public school preparation is second-rate. Many of those blacks who might have entered the profession were forced to attend such schools even after the 1954 *Brown* decision.

It was obvious as early as the seventies that it would take a two-pronged approach to find a way out of this dilemma. The first was to build supports to retain and graduate the limited number of blacks who qualified for entry. The second was to mount a frontal attack on the public institutions that prepared students, thereby enlarging the pool of eligible students (Gordon, 1988, p. 69).

As one reads the segment on minorities in the NSF journal, it becomes clear that the National Science Foundation realized that academic preparation, not disinterest, was the basis of the low participation rate. As an influential arm of government I was certain that they lobbied for greater governmental support for preparatory programs. But this did not happen. Poor and inner-city youths remained the least educated Americans.

To appreciate the overwhelming presence of whites in the engineering field in the seventies or, conversely, the absence of all others, consider that blacks represented only 1.5 percent of all science and engineering professionals while Asians represented 1.75 percent and all other minorities accounted for less than 1 percent as reported by the National Science Foundation (NSF, 1979, p. 136).

Chapter 8

The Eighties

During the 1980s several reports were produced that affirmed what many in the black communities had sensed: the ratio of white to minority citizens was rapidly changing. Many of the new minorities were not black, but by no stretch of the imagination could they be called white. They were Laotian, Vietnamese, Jamaican, Haitian, and on and on from places we had known only from geography classes or the wars. They came with differing languages and skills, but nearly all arrived with the belief that here they could educate their children.

Three demographic studies were published at this time and each was quite informative in terms of minority participation in the national economy and, by extrapolation, the fields of technologies. The first, *The Future of Work*, was reported in the August 9, 1983, edition of *USA Today*. This report forecast a workplace with widely separated levels of participation, managers, and low-level functionaries. When the AFL-CIO read the report it commented that there would not be enough high-tech jobs for workers currently losing their positions to robots and machines, much less enough employment to absorb the new workforce entrants. In other words, it was senseless to spread the net of acceptance to new populations. The status quo should remain.

In another article by Robert Kuttner in the July 1983 issue of *The Atlantic Monthly*, the workforce needs of the next decade were spelled out. Among the most prominent needs were those for 12,000 computer programmers and 125,000 more electrical engineers. Both categories bode well for black students interested in these technologies.

By far the most revealing report was that prepared by Ian McNett for the American Council of Education, the Forum of Educational Organization Leaders, and the Institute for Educational Leadership. The report was entitled *Demographic Imperatives: Implications for Educational Policy.* It was delivered on June 8, 1983. Among the findings and predictions were the following:

a. The new baby boom is reversing the decline in birth rates and is beginning to reverse the decline in school enrollment.

b. The over-65 population now outnumbers teenagers.

c. The average age of the white population is growing older; that of the minority population is much younger.

d. Minorities constitute the majority of school enrollments in twenty-three of twenty-five of the nation's largest cities.

e. By the year 2000, fifty-three major cities will have a majority minority population.

f. Population and education enrollments are continuing to shift from the Frost Belt to the Sun Belt.

g. Hispanics are the most urbanized group, with 88 percent living in cities, but more blacks live in inner cities than any other population group (71 percent).

h. Black and Hispanic participation in education diminishes drastically at higher levels.

i. The majority of blacks and Hispanics in higher education are enrolled in community colleges or predominantly black and Hispanic institutions.

j. Serious erosion has occurred in the rates of black and Hispanic high school graduates who go on to college.

k. Eighty percent of all black Ph.D.'s and 76 percent of Hispanic Ph.D.'s are in education and the social sciences.

l. Population and education trends could perpetuate the racial and ethnic divisions of American society.

m. The recent emphasis on science and technology may increase minority underrepresentation in high-income, high-prestige jobs.

n. High technology and other economic changes also threaten the white- and blue-collar middle class with loss of jobs and status.

o. Some projections forecast a truly high-tech future (i.e., requiring higher-order skills and paying well) for only a small portion of Americans.

p. Conflicts may result from the aging of the majority population and the youthfulness of the minority population.

q. Personal and national self-interest requires that the majority population address the needs of the minorities: for example, the retirement income of people at work today will depend on the productive employment of minority young people who are in school today, as will the future economy and the military. (McNett, 1983, p. 4)

McNett's comprehensive investigation was presented to a distinguished panel of governmental, industrial, and business leaders. The message was well understood but the task of reform to meet the needs was slow to develop.

While industrialists and business leaders prepared an attack on the much needed reforms, blacks aggressively positioned themselves with programs to radically change their representation in major fields. Working with selected industries and institutions, programs and organizations specifically designed to target young blacks were formed throughout the nation. Three organizations moved quickly to leadership roles in this effort. They were the National Society of Black Engineers (NSBE), the National Action Council for Minorities In Engineering (NACME), and the National Association of Minority Engineering Program Administrators (NAMEPA). These three organizations became the lobbyists, the advocates, and the underwriters of many of today's programs that recruit, retain, and graduate black engineers.

These three organizations combined can account for more than 90 percent of all black engineering students in the nation. Their numbers, disciplines, institutions, and graduation rates have become part of the data base for these organizations. Annual conferences, industrial support, summer internships, financial aid, and national publications geared to specific topics of interest are all part of the services that these organizations provide. NAMEPA produces an annual *Data Book* that compiles statistics from seventy-seven of the nation's top engineering schools.

Since the establishment of these supportive groups, the number of black engineers has steadily increased. As a comparison of the effectiveness of these groups we can examine the graduation rates of Howard University from 1935 to 1960, when 655 engineering and architecture degrees were granted; or we can look at the entire fifty-five years of service from 1910 to 1965, when a total of 714 degrees were granted. That total number rose to more than 3150 by 1986. Without the supportive organizations, increases in graduation rates would have been difficult to achieve. Only eleven of the first 714 degrees were granted to women, and this was at a time when 75 percent of all black engineers attended Howard (Wilkinson, 1961, p. 210). Now, with wider access and greater organizational support, more than 2000 blacks will graduate in the 1990–1991 class from schools throughout the nation. Among the black graduates there will be seventy women, a number 40 percent higher than the 1989–1990 figure of fifty.

Howard has continued to be one of the primary producers of black engineers. In 1987 it awarded 129 bachelor's degrees and thirty-four master's degrees in engineering (Black Issues, 1988, p. 17). A further comparison can be made by using the *NAMEPA Data Book*. For 1988 it showed 1315 blacks graduating from these 77 institutions and the 1989 edition showed 1581 (NAMEPA, 1989).

While blacks were increasing their numbers in the fields of engineering, whites have found new areas of opportunity. Banking, high finance, investment, and other forms of commerce have begun to siphon off those white students who once sought engineering as a life's work. If a comparison is made between the graduation rates of engineering students and those graduating with degrees in business and management over the sixteen-year period from 1971 to 1987, much is revealed.

In 1971, 50,000 engineering degrees were granted, and roughly 114,000 degrees in business and management. In 1971 women earned only 0.8 percent of the engineering degrees, while they earned 9.1 percent of the business and management degrees. This could lead an observer to conclude that women were opting for fields other than the male bastion of engineering. By 1981 engineering degrees had increased by 18,000 to 68,000, while business and management degrees increased by 71,000. That widening disparity in the choice of majors continued until 1986 when engineering degrees reached 95,000 and business and management degrees reached 238,000 (U.S. Department of Commerce, 1990, p. 162).

The next year, 1987, engineering degrees declined to 93,000—a significant drop at a time when technical expertise was sorely needed by American firms. Business degrees rose in 1987 and women earned nearly half of those degrees, 46.5 percent. Women earned only 13.7 percent of the engineering degrees in 1987. This becomes even more significant when you realize that these two disciplines accounted for 330,000 of the 991,000 degrees granted in 1987 (U.S. Department of Commerce, 1990, p. 162). Add to that the insult of wage differences—white men earned more than any other segment of the industry, more than white women, blacks, or Asians (NSF, 1979, p. 235).

It is interesting to note that as we discuss the plight of blacks wishing to enter the fields of engineering, we hear similar concerns and protests by women. They too have suffered a great deal of exclusion. WEPAN (Women In Engineering Program Advocates Network), a group designed to advocate women's equity in engineering, is now asking for programs of support similar to those blacks have established (Wilson, 1991, p. A27). Interesting, too, is the similarity in anecdotal complaints of institutional harassment and neglect recounted by women.

With white American males and females deserting engineering while Asian nations were making strong bids to become the technological leaders of the world, Americans turned to groups of Americans not normally thought of as contributors to the field of technology. Overtures of inclusion went out to blacks, women, hispanics, and native Americans. The erosion of the idea that engineering could remain the province of white males in a time when America was receiving a great influx of ethnic and racial minorities was being tested in the eighties.

Industrialists, anxious to find bodies and minds to fill vacant positions, sought out engineering schools and organizations that supported nonwhite engineering students. For groups such as NAMEPA, NSBE, and NACME this new validation and industrial support was warmly welcomed.

To add to the despair of American technology, the scientific knowledge of American 17-year-olds had taken a dangerous slide. A 1988 report issued by the Educational Testing Service under a mandate from the U.S. Congress showed that only 7 percent of America's 17-year-olds could succeed in college science courses (Black Issues, 1988, p. 25). Further reading of the report shows that when compared with the scores of thirteen competing academically advanced nations, the United States was consistently outpaced by Japan, Hong Kong, Sweden, England, and Singapore. Each of these nations is vying with the United States for technological superiority. The U.S. students ranked thirteenth in biology, eleventh in chemistry, and ninth in physics (Black Issues, 1988, p. 24).

By 1983 large college engineering programs began aggressively to seek out smaller institutions to form alliances that would allow students to attend liberal arts colleges to get the basic academic tools for engineering. Often the student could receive the equivalent of the first two years of the engineering degree at these colleges. Then, under the agreement with the larger engineering school, the student would be admitted as a sophomore or a junior and continue his/her education.

For the larger schools, this was an ideal situation. The smaller schools served as screens for the students, eliminating those who were poorly prepared for the academic challenge and strengthening the marginal students. For black students these new collegiate affiliations proved to be a boon for those who had come from less than adequate school districts. Often the smaller school was a community college, the institution most often chosen by blacks as their initial entry into postsecondary education. Here the pace could be slower and the cost far less than at an engineering school. Usually the community college was close to home, the cost was minimal, and the academic remediation and strengthening were integral parts of the community college mandate.

The combinations that resulted from these affiliations left no doubt about the cross-fertilization that was taking place in many of the schools of engineering. As an example, when one looks at the list of institutions affiliated with the Georgia Institute of Technology, one sees the traditional schools of the region; many were once all-white institutions. Also listed among its affiliates were Clark College, Morehouse College, and Morris Brown College, all of Atlanta, Georgia. In addition there is Tougaloo College of Tougaloo, Mississippi, and North Carolina Central College of Durham, North Carolina, both out-of-state schools; and finally, Spelman College, an all-women's school. These six institutions are among the many traditionally black colleges that are located in the South.

A new sophistication was evident in the many supportive programs that flourished in the 1980s. Programs that intervened as early as the elementary grades along with the continuing collegiate programs were introduced by schools of engineering and school districts in partnerships with public and private sector interests. Among the more successful schools employing the early intervention strategies, at least four have outstanding records. They are Georgia Tech, Northwestern, Cornell, and the University of California at Berkeley.

Georgia Tech initiated the Minority Introduction to Engineering (MITE) program in 1957 as a method of introducing black students to the field of engineering. The results of this effort are evident twenty years later in the number of black students graduating from the school's programs. Statistics compiled by the Engineering Manpower Commission show that Georgia Tech awarded fifty-one bachelor's degrees, twenty-five master's degrees, and one doctorate to blacks in 1987 (Farrell, 1988, p. 13). In 1988 and 1989 more than 100 blacks received their bachelor's degrees from this institution (NAMEPA, 1988, 1989). Among the supportive services offered by programs such as MITE are:

Academic Services

Math/science problem-solving workshops
Study skills workshops
Summer bridge programs
Tutoring

Counseling

Academic advising
Personal (financial aid)

Scholarships

Student Centers

Employment

Industry presentations/speakers
Industry tours
Résumé preparation

High School Outreach

Presentations, tours, workshops
Summer programs

Junior High School Outreach

Presentations, tours, workshops
Summer programs

On the collegiate level these programs could be found in nearly every state, often underwritten by state grants. In 1986 California had twenty-nine such programs while North Carolina, one of the states attempting to equalize engineering education, had only six. But while the twenty-nine California programs accounted for 1188 black students, the six North Carolina programs enrolled 1169 with the vast majority, 728, attending North Carolina A&T University (NACME, 1986, p. 52).

In 1986 the Engineering Manpower Commission of the American Association of Engineering Societies published a Fall report that identified schools that had enrolled the largest number of black students for the 1986–1987 academic year. Of the top eleven schools, seven were historically black colleges and universities (HBCUs). For blacks interested in engineering, this was indeed a triumph. With access to the more famous institutions in the North and West, most black undergraduates were choosing schools that promised the additional comfort of racial acceptance. As this report was being readied for publication, racial incidents on the nation's campuses were escalating. In the North and West reports of harassment, racial slurs, denigrating graffiti, and physical confrontations were not uncommon. In 1985 incidents had become so common on the campuses of California's public colleges and universities that a conference of minority students and legislators was scheduled for October 5, 1988, at the UCLA campus. After listening to hours of student complaints, state senator Art Torres (D–Los Angeles) said, "It cannot be denied that racial incidents destroy the very core of the institution and tear at the moral fabric of the university and the society as a whole" (Blau, 1988, p. 22). The complaints came not only from the Los Angeles campus but from Berkeley, Santa Cruz, and Santa Barbara as well.

Among the top eleven colleges listed in the Commission report are Prairie View A&M, Southern University, North Carolina A&T, Howard University, Tuskegee University, Tennessee State, and Morgan University. In 1986 these seven black HBCUs enrolled more than 4800 black engineering students. This is significant, also, because by 1986 black students could attend any school for which they qualified. They have continued to choose several HBCU engineering programs and to graduate. Since 1973–1974, several southern schools have graduated an average of forty to fifty black engineering students per year—this, even when the controversy over testing was rampant (NACME, 1986).

Listed also in the Commission report were the top degree-grant-ing schools for blacks. Here again the HBCUs comprised six of the first ten schools listed in 1987. Howard led the list by granting 129 degrees to candidates while Tennessee State University ranked tenth, granting thirty-eight degrees (Black Issues, 1988, p. 21). The schools that once were among the few that graduated blacks (MIT, Yale, and Harvard) cannot be found on the list.

1990

The 1990 class of engineering graduates as forecast by the Engi-neering Manpower Commission will show the following totals:

Discipline	Total No. of Graduates	No. of Black Graduates	Percentage of Class
electrical	21385	1013	.047
mechanical	14969	506	.033
civil	7587	230	.03
chemical	3622	169	.04
computer	4355	164	.037
industrial	4306	245	.056
totals	56224	2327	.041

Source: Basta, 1990, p. 82.

The numbers are more dismal for the overall engineering com-munity than they are for blacks. As a result, black graduates will discover a job market that welcomes them. A review of the num-bers show a 6.7 percent drop in electrical/electronic and computer engineers, even though minority enrollments have increased in these specialties. Mechanical and industrial engineering, both growth majors in the early eighties, have begun to slide. Fortu-nately for the 1990 chemical engineering graduates, the downturn in engineering enrollments has removed some of the stress from the job search. Chemical engineers will not have to search far to find positions since their field is expanding and their enrollments have declined for the last six years. Civil engineering has suffered similar declines, with the 1990 class size down 25 percent since 1981. This is the most severe drop across the disciplines (Basta, 1991, p. 82). As a nation we can no longer allow our outmoded system of privilege to interfere with our survival. Economically as well as technically, we are rapidly losing our position as a leading world economy. Whether it is a high-tech toy, a car, or an electrical gadget, it is obvious that many of our purchases come from countries that threaten our position of prominence. But a greater threat is posed by our inability to redirect the one resource over which we have control, our human capital. The investment that must be made in our educational infrastructure and the will to commit the nation's capital to a long-range plan for educational revitalization seems lacking.

In addition, by the year 2000 our educational stock of 18-year-olds will have shrunk by 20 percent and one in every three will be black or hispanic. The ratio of worker to social security recipient will have narrowed from 16 to 1 in 1950 to 1 to 1 in the early twenty-first century (Kenmitzer, 1988, p. 88).

While majority Americans may find this forecast dismal, minority Americans with hope of gaining access to the mainstream may find this forecast laden with hope. If black Americans are to secure a place in engineering and technology in this country, this may be the moment.

Conclusions and Implications

CONCLUSIONS

It seems clear that there are two distinct eras in this 135-year-story of American blacks in the fields of technology. The first extends from Emancipation to 1950; the second covers 1950 to the present. The conclusions reached after reviewing the first eighty-five year span, 1865 to 1950, of this investigation reveals a persistent black population striving for representation in the engineering and technological arena of this country. Though there are times when economic peril, migratory disruption, the tyranny of the workplace, and racism imperil that striving, the will to succeed prevails.

This recounting uncovers incidents, papers, and converging pressures that served at times to inhibit the progress of black higher education in general and engineering and technological higher education in particular. On other occasions, those same pressures served to spur the black community to action.

Over this eighty-five year span, it is obvious that there is a glaring disparity between the representation of blacks in the American population and the number of black Americans in these specialized areas. This research stands not as an excuse for this disparity; rather, it serves to explain the patterns of American higher education and of the greater society that aided in producing this disparity.

This research leads to the following conclusions:

1. There exists a record of the contributions of black Americans in the areas of engineering, technology, and other improvements in the general welfare of the country. This record is continuous throughout the period. Yet these contributions are, for the most part, missing from the traditional sources for our understanding of American history; and the practice of overlooking, ignoring, or forgetting these contributions has effectively denied millions of Americans a true sense of their heritage.

2. The engineering profession evolved, during the nineteenth century, from a trade in which apprentices and tinkers could learn on the job to a profession in which formal training and advanced education were essential to certification. In this process, black Americans were systematically subjected to a number of practices of exclusion from such training and education that effectively prevented them from entering into the engineering and technological fields. The consequence of these practices include denying these Americans the status and professional opportunity that their white contemporaries had, while at the same time denying their country the chance to grow and benefit from their intelligence and invention.

3. Institutions of higher education, both northern and southern, engaged in exclusionary practices: These ranged from the denial of on-campus housing, exclusion from campus activities and groups, and from academic and professional organizations; and a general lack of institutional support, to (particularly in the South) outright refusal of admission.

4. In the South there was an unwillingness in some states to provide substantial postsecondary technical education throughout this period. The founding of North Carolina Agricultural and Technical College (NCA&T) is an example of the form of this exclusion. NCA&T was founded by the state as a condition for receiving funds for its segregated institution, North Carolina Agricultural and Mechanical University (NCA&M), under the terms of the Morrill Act. NCA&M was an engineering school that assured the state's white students of an engineering education within the

state's boundaries; the black school did not become an engineering school until four decades after its founding.

5. Many states in the South employed voucher systems that forced blacks to travel north to do advanced work in many fields, and particularly for technical educations. The complexity of the voucher system, devised to preserve the segregated status of publicly funded colleges, is interpreted as an attempt to dissuade rather than encourage black participation at all levels of the educational system. This contributed to the paucity of black Americans with appropriate engineering and technological degrees during this period.

6. The apparent manipulation of black leaders by public officials at all levels was another strategy of exclusion and oppression during this period. Booker T. Washington is cited as an example of this tactic; Washington's acceptance and elevation by men of power gave him leadership among black Americans. At the same time, his conservative position on social issues, especially on the role and form of education for blacks, served to diffuse and even discredit the protests and proposals from other sectors of the black community. This anointment by the powerful served notice that there was a mode of conduct and a level of aspiration that would be rewarded. Conversely, there were modes of conduct and levels of aspiration that would be ignored.

IMPLICATIONS OF THIS STUDY

The initial section of this research covers a period of time that ended forty years ago, but the aftershocks of the material are still felt throughout the nation; and more especially within the small, technologically oriented community of American industry. The implications that one may draw from this exercise are many, but they are determined by the view one takes of the evidence that has been presented. If one views all of this as a benign confluence of events without evil intent, then the likelihood is that one will see black Americans as being justly denied the right to full participation in the mainstream of American life. If, on the other hand, one takes the position that a concerted effort was made to deny blacks their constitutional guarantees of the right to life, liberty, and the pursuit of happiness, then the plot that worked with remarkable success has deprived black citizens far beyond the span of this volume.

This second position leads to the belief that the logical extension of this denial was the refusal by the states to provide equal educational facilities for blacks. This denial was all-inclusive; it went from the elementary grades through postsecondary options. When the courts decreed and the media affirmed that the treatment that blacks received was lawful, it was eagerly accepted. The resulting anger and mistrust of these early decisions still divide the races.

Whether one takes the first or second view of the events or any of the many positions that lie between the two poles, the legacy of this period has meant that substantial ground has been lost in the technological marketplace, not only by black citizens but by the country as a whole. In the last thirty-five or forty years attempts have been made to correct the damages done, but the effort has come at a time when most of the educationally oppressed have lost faith in the system. Consequently, this task has been made even more formidable by the long neglect.

We now face a time when no contribution to the general welfare can be shunned, for we are slipping from our national leadership position in the world of technology. Add to that the great influx of foreign immigrants of every hue and dialect and we see that the need to promote tolerance is more critical now than ever. As Americans, we are a people for whom intolerance has been a way of life; and now we are forced, by numbers and a fear of economic failure, to adopt a new and radically different policy toward other peoples and races.

The demographics of American society, more than the generosity of love and charity, are driving this new wave of acceptance. It is industry, more than the religious community, that has awakened this new sense of fair play, and that now preaches a sermon of plurality and coexistence.

As mentioned earlier, the threat of and participation in two world wars was not enough to break the barriers to equal higher education. The potential loss of leadership and revenues appear to have superior persuasive powers.

As a result, colleges and universities have become more accepting of students who do not fit the established mold and who are different from their customary alumni. Programs in areas of greatest national need are now commonplace on campuses throughout the country. This is true in every region of the country. Programs in engineering with overt invitations to black students can be found as readily in Florida as in New York.

It is reasonable to assume that there would have been no change in attitude had our position of leadership not been threatened or if our ability to prosper had continued. Black Americans see this as clearly as their white fellow citizens and though they are beginning to respond to the opportunities, they approach these opportunities with full knowledge that theirs is something less than a wholehearted welcome. The years of segregation and educational denial have left a national market that must employ them skeptical of their ability to produce the same quality of work as their white coworkers.

If one is searching for the downside of the new liberalism, it is to be found in the inability of some citizens to abandon the long-cultivated view of the black American. It is difficult to abandon those deeply held stereotypes of the "shiftless lout" who now claims to be the equal of white engineers. It is equally difficult for many black Americans to accept this new opportunity because they, too, have come to believe that they would be overstepping their bounds if they were to compete with whites for traditional "white" jobs. In this manner the country as a whole suffers from the early mismanagement of its educational and social obligations to a segment of its population.

There is no evidence that additional technical input would not have benefited America, the South, or the individual enterprises. Truly, the century-plus span of this investigation shows that there was never an overabundance of engineers or technical expertise. There was never a time when America could not have used the inventiveness of all of its citizens; but the educational plan of the nation excluded a large segment of the population, thereby limiting the volume of black input and the number of those blacks who had access to the system. It is fair to say that any contributions from blacks were unwanted.

For Americans, starting with Thomas Jefferson, who over the years have come to know and respect the relationship between democracy, citizenship, and popular education, this is a story of institutional tyranny. Jefferson argued before the Virginia Legislature in 1787 for the provision of a popular education system that offered entry-level education to every white child of the Commonwealth and then the opportunity for the brightest male students to proceed as far as their talents would allow including college opportunities. This, if enacted, would have meant that 40 percent of the state's juvenile population, the children of slaves, was ignored (Anderson, 1988, p. 1). Jefferson's pleas were both sexist and racist, but in 1787 he was able to hold his audience and attempt to make his case.

This story begins nearly one hundred years later and tells of many of the same people being denied the basic rights of a democracy. It is obvious that a bond exists between education and citizenship and that any abridgement of the first means that one's participation in the second, the democratic process, is severely limited.

As we look back with the advantage of time and the wisdom wrought of the struggle, it is easy to see that the policies and practices of the late nineteenth and early twentieth centuries were poorly formulated. The last forty years have only made crystalline the many previous claims of discrimination. The blame for those policies can be placed at many doors, but placing of blame should now become secondary to finding a remedy for the problem. The struggle for parity in education has been an ongoing American saga for more than a century and a quarter. The need for parity and the moral imperatives that should have propelled the nation toward its sworn goals have always been evident—they are today. As a nation and a people, we have chosen to ignore our constitutional mandate and regard basic education as a privilege rather than a right.

As a result we now find ourselves being threatened by nations one half or one quarter our size—and we are losing. Unfortunately this is not a contest that we can lose today with the hope of winning another contest tomorrow. A loss in the technological contest of the late twentieth or early twenty-first century will certainly mean that we shall be a permanent second-class industrial nation. Disagreements centered around gender, race, class, or ethnicity must be submerged and a new Americanism must be forged that will embrace and enhance all citizens. Our school systems need major repairs. The field upon which our academic games are played must be leveled so that young people from the least fortunate circumstances have an equal opportunity to contribute to the general welfare of the nation. Curriculum reform along with retention inducements must become standard fare if we are to retain students in our schools.

But even if all of the reforms are made, curricula revamped, and divisive issues put to rest, there remains a larger, more urgent question. I fear it is one that is too seldom asked—too often avoided. Since 1960 overtures to minorities, blacks in particular, have been plentiful for entry into the fields of engineering. Barriers to entry have been abolished. Supportive services have been erected in their place. All of the inducements have been given, but should blacks succumb to the offer? That is the overriding question.

As we look at the American black community today we can see many gaps in the racial infrastructure. Health care, dental expertise, education, construction—all are crying for involvement of the brightest black minds. A strong case can be made for blacks to turn from the technologies as have whites, even though their motivations may be different. A black doctor in an urban setting does far more to sustain his race on a day-to-day basis than any engineer.

It is a fact that one in every three American engineers is in some way connected to a program of national defense. Blacks, with even a short command of military history, realize that for the last forty years America has fought only enemies of color: southeast Asians,

Granadians, Panamanians, and Iraqis. In the future, this could be a factor in the choice of majors for minority students.

Black Americans need to have their own agenda for racial progress. Perhaps engineering is a part of the total thrust for the race, but it should not be seen as the major focus of the effort. Blacks continue to need scholars in many fields. A truly level playing field would allow for greater choice and a wider disperse-ment of talent. The generous offers of scholarship and academic support for engineering students must be broadened to include those who wish, with equal zeal, to teach kindergarten or become city planners. In many black urban neighborhoods these two disciplines could conceivably do more to improve the general welfare than engineering could.

In the end America must find the resolve to build a national machine that can compete in the international market of technol-ogy. But that machine must be built with input from all of our communities. If this can be done, we can begin to believe that the nation has begun the long climb toward equality of opportunity in the fields of technology and engineering. Still, the distance that we must travel in search of parity means that this will be a long and arduous task to accomplish. At the same time, black Americans must map out a strategy that promotes their interests. It is highly unlikely that two such divergent goals can find harmony.

Appendix A

Diamond Scope, Journal of Howard University School of Engineering, Fall 1985

Diamond Scope

75 Years of Engineering Education Excellence

SCHOOL OF ENGINEERING   HOWARD UNIVERSITY   Fall '85

A Prologue

A little more than 50 years ago, facing a climate of economic austerity, many colleges and universities were dismantling their engineering curricula. Nowhere were these pressures felt more strongly than at Howard, when in 1933, the Howard University Board of Trustees approved a recommendation abolishing courses in Architecture, Electrical, Civil and Mechanical Engineering at the end of the 1933-34 academic year.

Dr. Lewis King Downing, then head of the Department of Architecture and Engineering under the auspices of the School of Applied Sciences, quickly dispatched a letter to Dr. Mordecai Johnson, president of Howard University, to protest this edict. The first point in Downing's letter was the fact that this divestiture would result, at best, in negligible savings to the University.

This argument, however, was only the tip of the iceberg. Fiscal loss could never touch the *heart* of the matter. And Dean Downing knew the heart of the matter with a certainty. What Downing hoped to maintain had a greater value than could be monetarily assigned — what he was defending was the conservation of the future of many individuals, and even, as he saw it, the future of an entire people. In his letter he stated, "Education today must be direct, compact, and, while never brief, should be very practical to be of future value. Law, Engineering, Medicine and Architecture are consistent with this principle. No race of people in America is more economically barren than the Negro." He declared that

there was a "much needed development among our race of a greater appreciation for technical work and its services to man in the establishment of a people upon a sound economic basis." Nor did he limit his vision — his appeal was broad: "No person of reasonable intelligence and judgement can discount the work of the engineer and architect in present-day civilization . . . the work of the scientist can mean little if it cannot be moulded into a utility whether practical or artistic. That is the business of the engineer or architect, whether he be white or black."

Inspiration begets boldness. Downing's vision for the future of blacks in engineering and architectural professions gave him the audacity not only to argue for continuation of these programs, but to assert that their significance warranted the creation of a separate School of Engineering and Architecture!

To Downing's voice was added that of William P. Cannady, president of the Howard University Engineering Society, who, in a measured but impassioned letter to the Trustees, wrote that "the complete loss in the final analysis will be greater than any immediate saving." The fight to retain engineering programs was joined by the National Technical Association. Mr. John A. Lankford of the national NTA forwarded to the H.U. administration the findings of a NTA committee which strongly recommended continuing these programs, citing the fact that "during the past 21 years . . . the race has been educated to the possibilities of these professions . . . industrial leaders have learned of the technical capabilities of the

Negro..." and questioning, "Is it good business to throw away such an investment that has proved successful?"

As we know, Engineering and Architecture not only won a reprieve from extinction, but Dean Downing's faith was validated—in 1934 the School of Engineering and Architecture was established as a separate school in recognition of the distinct importance of these professions.

Thus, a little more than 25 years later in 1960, Downing appointed a committee chaired by Howard H. Mackey to plan for the 50th anniversary of the school that was almost abolished. The committee included Stephen S. Davis, Addison E. Richmond, Walter T. Daniels, Ernest R. Welch, James Webster, Darnley E. Howard, Leon Brown, Leroy J.H. Brown, Arthur F. Moore, Jr., James Overby, and Frederick B. Wilkinson. On the occasion of the 50th anniversary banquet on June 8, 1961, plaques were presented to the following faculty members for distinguished service: Lewis K. Downing (Civil-40 years), Howard H. Mackey (Architecture-40 years), Darnley Howard (Mechanical-35 years), Ernest R. Welch (Electrical-35 years) and Addison E. Richmond (Civil-30 years). Mr. F.D. Wilkinson, administrative assistant, was honored

for writing the history of the school, *Fifty Years of Engineering and Architecture at Howard University.*

The gift of time has wrought many changes in the School, including new degree programs and expanded research activities. And, of course, the challenge of preserving the School's historical mission, has passed to another generation. Among our retired faculty, those who still inspire us with their interest in the school's welfare are professors *emeriti* Walter T. Daniels, Addison E. Richmond, James Webster, Francis Steele, and Raymond Jones. Death has also diminished our ranks—we remember with affection the gifts of those who enriched the school: Lewis K. Downing, Stephen S. Davis, Priscilla S. Gray, Ernest R. Welch, Clifton B. Samuels, William Taylor and Lee J. Purnell.

Dean. M. Lucius Walker, has rightly stated that "we owe a debt of gratitude to the School's pioneers through whose lifelong commitment, the School survived many perilous moments in its history." Thanks to their faith, persistence, and vision, we are now observing our Diamond Jubilee and can plan to leave a legacy for those who will celebrate the centennial of Engineering Education at Howard University in the year 2000.

Source: Leatha S. Mitchell, "A Prologue," originally published in *Diamond Scope* by Howard University, School of Engineering. Used by permission.

Appendix B

An Information Sheet from L. K. Downing of Howard University to George Davis, Hampton Institute, February 28, 1944

HAMPTON INSTITUTE
HAMPTON, VIRGINIA

DIVISION OF TRADES AND INDUSTRIES
To: Howard University

February 28,1944

Gentlemen:

Please furnish us with the following information:

DEPARTMENT	VALUE OF LAB. EQUIP.	OTHER EQUIP. SUCH AS PHYSICS, CHEM., ETC.	VALUE OF BUILDINGS	OTHER ITEMS	ENROLL-MENT
Architecture	$5,800.00				17
Civil Engineering	15,600.00				28
Electrical Eng.	22,100.00				37
Mechanical Eng.	28,900.00				41
Physics		$22,200.00			
Chemistry		208,000.00			
Mathematics		1,560.00			
Engineering & Arch. Building			$23,000.00		
Thirkield (Part)			10,400.00		
Clarke H.(Part)			23,370.00		

L. K. Downing
Howard University

Source: Courtesy of Hampton University Archives.

A Letter from Ovid Eshbach of
Northwestern University to George
Davis of Hampton Institute,
March 10, 1944

NORTHWESTERN UNIVERSITY
EVANSTON, ILLINOIS

THE TECHNOLOGICAL INSTITUTE   March 10, 1944

Mr. George W. Davis, Acting Director,
Division of Trades and Industries
Hampton Institute
Hampton, Virginia

Dear Mr. Davis:

I am pleased to answer your inquiry of February 23. The cost of
laboratory equipment in the several departments of the Institute is
approximately as follows:

                General Equipment $280,000
                Chemistry 250,000
                Chemical Engineering   60,000
                Civil Engineering 125,000
                Electrical Engineering 130,000
                Mechanical Engineering 120,000
                Physics. 200,000
                                              $1,165,000

The cost of the building housing these departments, which includes
such equipment as chemistry tables, power plant, and other attached
apparatus, is $4,500,000. The normal enrollment in each department
is as follows:

                Civil Engineering . . . . 100 - 150
                Mechanical Engineering . . . . . 200 - 250
                Chemical Engineering . . . . . . 200 - 250
                Electrical Engineering . . . . . 150 - 200

Chemistry, which includes 300 engineers, has a normal total enrollment of 900. Physics, which also includes about 300 engineers, has
a normal enrollment of 700. The average yearly expense of teaching
an engineering student is approximately $600.

                        Yours sincerely,

                        Ovid W. Eshbach

                        Ovid W. Eshbach
OWE:JMS   Dean

Source: Courtesy of Hampton University Archives

Appendix D

=====

"Considerations and
Recommendations for the Future
Curriculum for Trades and
Industries at Hampton Institute"

P. V. Jewell, Professor of Engineering,
Tennessee A & I State College,
Nashville, Tennessee

I. CONSIDERATIONS
        The history, reputation and resource of Hampton
Institute are good. The history and reputation are such that
Hampton Institute should expect an increase in enrollment in male
students as soon as the war emergency is over. The financial
reputation of Hampton Institute is apparently of fine shape, but
there is no evidence in sight of immediate large gifts which
could suggest any injudicious program of development for the
department of trades and industries. The past and present
programs seem to imply that the division of trades and industries
is well equipped to train students for craft occupations in the
technical institute level as well as for certain elementary trade
levels. In general it may be said, based on the judgement of Mr.
Tulberry that certain facilities and equipment at Hampton compare
favorably with those at other technical institutes as well as
Wentworth Institute.

        The trend in trades and in industries, if a short
period of twenty years may be termed a trend, seem to imply that
the outstanding workman must be well equipped with a higher
backlog of related knowledge. It was quoted considerably that
Hampton Institute might concern itself with the development of
outstanding trade and industrial workers rather than casual
competitive training, hitting through the usual skill bracket.
The trends in industrial education also seem to carry an
increased emphasis on technical education. Industrial education
now includes skill programs and problems in economics and is
woven with certain distributive occupations. If Hampton
Institute is to keep abreast of such a trend, it is suggested
that the curriculum be so constructed as to form some plan for
the teaching industries and economics which will be prerequisite
to job-handling and advancement if not a prerequisite to job
getting in a tight labor market.

        It seems to be the consensus of opinion the training of
Negro youth in the field of industrial education in the area
which Hampton serves is still deficient. It is expected that
congress will eventually pass the bill for aid to vocational
education. With this in view it appears unwise to act in program
formulating with precipitate action. Even with $100,000,000.00
or thereabouts to be spent in the United States the actual
amount devoted to the southern area is small and the expected
proportion in any state to be devoted to Negroes will certainly
not be above the ratio of that population to the total population
even at best. My experience suggests that the states will apply
that "trickle" to the lowest level of industrial training. Its
ultimate application will probably be in industrial arts and

introductory trade training. This will leave the field of
vocational technical education, entrepreneurs of small
enterprises, junior engineering, modern building, construction,
maritime engineering and so forth unprovided for. Tuskeegee will
certainly go in heavily for aviation. Hampton might lead in
maritime training. Contrary to the opinion of the majority of
the group which was writing the report to you, I feel that it
would be injudicious to expand Hampton's heritage for a moss of
pottage--competition with the federal-state vocational work by
lowering standards of instruction or admission. A critical study
of admission requirements to colleges in the area which Hampton
Institute serves would probably show less than six elective units
out of fifteen or sixteen admission units. It is recommended
that Hampton determine what these basic ten requirements are for
her whole institution. Then do not waive them for any student.
The vocational technical department might waive a total of not
more than one half the electives or even all the electives for
special cases. Regardless of entrance requirements i would
question the judiciousness of spreading all over the field of
industrial training.

        Apprenticeship training for Negroes in the broad field
of trade and industries is limited in its availability. It does
appear to me that the Alumni Association of Hampton Institute
with its diversified experiences and accomplishments might well
afford to attack the program of providing some apprenticeship
training either with the craft industries which they have created
or with the industry of which they are a part. The program of
American Labor Unions must be investigated for the division of
trades and industries at Hampton Institute. The curriculum must
be expanded to give functional training and experience in the
labor unions. This suggests that a person skilled in labor
programs be added to the staff to give vocational guidance along
that line. Said person should understand from the inside all the
implications of Labor and interpret the main point of view as it
will be unfolded in Schellenback's program. Negro youth must be
warned of the aids and abuses of union activities. All too often
minority groups clutch at promises made on emotion rather than
reason.

II. RECOMMENDATIONS

    1. For a four year period no specific offerings should be
eliminated from the present program of the division of trades and
industries. However, during the four year period every offering
must be thoroughly scrutinized, each job must be analyzed, and
the curriculum re-organized to meet changes made necessary by
change of time. It is my judgement that these courses be so
planned as to require of any given students the substantial
equivalent of a high school education. This does not necessarily
mean that a diploma will be required but it does suggest that the
students will be tested and advised concerning his qualifications
in many areas of training. Each student should meet all
requirements for freshmen but not necessarily all elective

requirements.

2. It is recommended that the building trade courses require more knowledge of certain metals and new materials and methods. Trade requirements should be revised to include an increased amount of fundamental economics, more emphasis must be placed on quantity surveys and skills for handling men. These areas have been Hampton's outstanding contribution for over four decades.

3. It is recommended that Hampton consider very seriously entering into the field of naval-maritime work during this episode of the world war. Negroes have been readmitted for the first time to the navy significantly in about one hundred years. It is my belief that the American Merchant Marine may also find some use for Negro youth. A study of the same might prove of value. If Hampton is going to meet the needs of students on her campus it might be well to study for a while the preparation of some workers in the field of general engineering after the pattern of Swarthmore College.

4. It is my belief that the states will improve training in the area of industrial arts and vocational education at the lowest level. I believe that Hampton might well afford to step up its requirements for admission to the higher level properly in the terms of the job she proposes to do. If the states ever increase their elementary requirements and do a thorough job at the lowest level it might not seem the better part of judgement for the institute to enter into direct competition. It might be a useful purpose of Hampton Institute to broaden its pattern for requirements and understanding of its industrial students so that the trade and industrial teachers might be in a position to train skilled workers who can also live in a twentieth community with some skill.

5. Like Charles Elliott, I believe in the value in education of the life career motive. Among poorer people this may produce strain. I would recommend that for the very entering day of the students some training in the life career of the student be provided. However, I also know that in living in the twentieth century there are certain general requirements which are common to all young people regardless of their field of employment. As early as possible I should like to see this common field of knowledge instituted for all students and have specialized programs intensified progressively. The function of guidance should be to view and review guidance in order that proper emphasis may be placed on those aspects of the general guidance that are general. This suggests that such subjects as freshman English, freshman mathematics and freshman science be hauled before a board of critical review. These courses should be studied in light of their end objectives in the applied field also. All too often the usual mathematics or science teacher however well prepared in the so-called "pure field" is not equipped unaided to serve the needs of the applied field of students. There is no question of principles but frequently due

to limited experience the usual mathematics or science teacher
provides insufficient emphasis in certain areas that are the very
"lifeblood of success" in some technical areas of gainful
employment.

        We further recommend that the whole program of guidance
be hauled before a critical board of review. The usually
academically trained guidance expert is very well equipped to do
group or rationalized program of a statistical nature in an
excellent manner. But all too frequently in the field of "pure"
guidance a highly trained specialist may be quite unaware of the
occupational requirements of articulated mental, digital and
technical skills that are prerequisite to satisfactory job
performance and living satisfaction of industrial and technical
workers. Such a specialist acting alone can hardly interpret the
meanings of test data for areas in which he has no experience at
all as a normal human employee. It must be borne in mind that
test data that have served the army and the navy have been geared
to the surety of success for the army and the navy. There is no
attempt of their desires to satisfy individual aptitudes, and
needs. They have proceeded on the assumption that the screen
reject rather than that the screen be used as an educational
device. It thus seems imperative that the vocational aspect of
guidance be placed in the guidance program for the Trade-
Industrial-Engineering program if guidance is to meet the needs
of the afore-mentioned division of instruction. The articulating
person must be informed of jobs and needs of the occupations and
must use the usual guidance technician to provide him with the
data he needs for interpretation and counseling individuals. The
proposed technical industrial coordinator should be able to
articulate the testers with the jobs if guidance is to become
functional rather than statistical. To this end actual training
and experience within industry appear more important than
formalized "credit getting."

                                Respectfully submitted,
                                    /a/per
                                P.V. Jewell
                                Professor in Engineering

Note: This correspondence has been retyped because of the poor quality of the copies
        provided.

Source: Courtesy of Hampton University Archives.

Appendix E

A Letter from Ralph Winslow of Rensselaer Polytechnic Institute to George Davis of Hampton Institute, March 11, 1944

RENSSELAER POLYTECHNIC INSTITUTE
DEPARTMENT OF ARCHITECTURE
TROY, NEW YORK

March 11, 1944

Mr. George W. Davis
Acting Director
Division of Trades and Industries
Hampton Institute
Hampton, Virginia

Dear Mr. Davis:

I am enclosing herewith the best answer that I can give you
to the questions you raised in your letter of February 28.

On the mimeographed sheet, which you enclosed with your letter,
I have listed the principle engineering departments and the
enrollment in each of these for the year 1940, which was a
typical year. As you know, our present enrollment under the
war training program has little significance. In addition to
the students listed on this sheet, there are others in the
departments of Biology, Physics, and Chemistry, graduate
students and special students in whom you would be less interested. Our total enrollment is normally around 1500.

Although I should like very much to help you in every way
and would be glad to set down detailed figures for the other
columns on your sheet, I find it impossible to break down
our total figures in such a way as to assess parts of them
against the various departments. The total value of our
buildings is very close to $5,500,000, and the value of
laboratory equipment is about $2,500,000. There is, however,
no building on the campus used exclusively by one department,
and most of the equipment is used by at least two and some-
times more departments.

However, I should like to make a suggestion which by-passes
the details and comes down to the essential nature of the
thing that you seem to have in mind. You state in your
letter that you would like to have this information so that
you can determine approximate costs of engineering courses
if, in the future, you find it necessary (or desirable) to
change the character of your instruction from the trade school
level to that of the technical institution or engineering
college. This statement of yours is really the entire story
underlying your desire for information, and it is this goal
that I should like to talk about.

Mr. George W. Davis   Page 2   March 11, 1944

First of all, I believe that you are wise and entirely sound
in considering this possible change. Furthermore, I think
that you should proceed with it to the best of your ability,
as soon as conditions, particularly your financial status,
warrant. Having decided upon this step in principle, the
most difficult task is now one of how to implement it. You
are obviously confronted with the problem of deciding on
which departments would draw the most students and would cost
the least to establish and maintain in terms of building and
equipment. I am afraid that this approach is a very difficult one and not altogether a wise one. I trust that you
will not object to a practical suggestion which may help you
to arrive at your goal more easily.

There are many liberal arts schools in this country and com-
paratively few schools of engineering. The trend of modern
civilization, accelerated by the impact of the war, has
enhanced the importance of the engineering schools, and some
of the liberal arts schools have felt seriously pinched.
These liberal arts schools are tending to change their curricula in order to make them more scientific and technical in
nature. It is not, however, the intention of these schools
to convert their status to that of technical schools. In
many cases, these schools are modifying their curricula so
as to provide students with pre-technical training of three
years length. At the end of this time, the student goes to
a technical school, already established with its buildings
and expensive equipment, and there he graduates in his chosen
engineering or scientific field and receives degrees from
both institutions. In order to accomplish this, an arrangement is made between the two schools concerned. The
Rensselaer Polytechnic Institute has such an arrangement with
Trinity College. The Massachusetts Institute of Technology
has a similar arrangement with Williams and Rutgers.

Now, after this long preamble, I come to my suggestion.
Your institution is not a liberal arts school of collegiate
standing. Nevertheless, I think that your position is some-
what the same with regard to the technical schools; the only
difference being that, if you entered upon such a plan, you
would not be able to grant a degree from your own institution,
and your students would receive degrees only from the technical school in which they finished.

I enclose, on a separate sheet, the Trinity College curriculum for this plan. Obviously, the student completes his
education at much less expense than would otherwise be the
case.

Mr. George W. Davis   Page 3   March 11, 1944

The advantages of this plan for the Hampton Institute are
many. You will be given an opportunity of building up stronger
courses in the basic sciences. You will be able to select
some of these students as they go through your hands and to
arrange to take them back on your faculty as instructors when
they have received their advanced training. You will be
slowly adding such pieces of laboratory equipment as will be
desirable for the teaching of chemistry and physics, and you
will be changing the character of your institution in the
direction which you now seem to have in mind. You will not
be required to go to any very great expense immediately in
trying to establish a full-blown department. Finally, when
this plan has been in operation for a number of years, you
will be in a much better position to take the final step;
that is, to establish one or two engineering departments,
since your equipment, curricula, and staff will then be ready
for such a development.

As a matter of fact, this is exactly what Trinity College
hopes to do. They have stated frankly that they will, if
it seems feasible, ultimately offer complete engineering
courses, leading to engineering degrees.

I regret very much not being able to give you the type of
information you ask for in your letter, but I hope that
you will find this material of some interest to you.

I wish you great success in your undertaking.

                    Sincerely yours,   -

                    Ralph E. Winslow

                    Ralph E. Winslow
                    Head of the Department

rew:sdo
Enclosures (2)

HAMPTON INSTITUTE
HAMPTON, VIRGINIA

DIVISION OF TRADES AND INDUSTRIES

February 28,1944

To: Rensselaer Polytechnic Institute

Gentlemen:

Please furnish us with the following information:

DEPARTMENT	VALUE OF LAB. EQUIP.	OTHER EQUIP. SUCH AS PHYSICS, CHEM., ETC.	VALUE OF BUILDINGS	OTHER ITEMS	ENROLL-MENT
Civil Engineering					110
Mechanical Engineering					250
Electrical Engineering					186
Chemical Engineering					276
Business Administration					165
Architecture					46
Aeroanutical Engineering					198
Industrial Engineering					89
Metallurgical Engineering					87

The work at Trinity College under the proposed plan would
follow the curriculum below:

FIRST YEAR

English
Chemistry
Physics
Mathematics
Engineering 1 (Engineering
          Drawing)

English
Chemistry
Physics I
Mathematics
Engineering 2 (Descriptive
          Geometry)

SECOND YEAR

Mathematics
Physics II (Mechanics & Heat)
Engineering 3 (Engineering
          Materials)
2 Electives

Mathematics
Physics II (Electricity)
Engineering 8 (Thermo. &
          Heat Power)
2 Electives

THIRD YEAR

Engineering 7 (Appl. Mechanics,
   Mechanisms & Elem. Machine Design
Engineering 10 (Physics 4)(Elements
   of Electrical Engineering)
3 Electives

Engineering 7

Engineering 10

3 Electives

The electives suggested cover courses in History, English,
Economics, Modern Language, Psychology, Philosophy. Some would
be used to satisfy Trinity's degree requirements.

Source: Courtesy of Hampton University Archives.

Bibliography

BOOKS AND JOURNAL ARTICLES

Allison, M. G. "The Year in Negro Education." *Crisis* (July 1920): 126.
Allison, M. G. "The Horizon" *Crisis* (January 1922): 120.
Ambrose, Stephen E. *Eisenhower, Vol. II: The President.* New York: Simon and Schuster, 1985.
Anderson, James D. *The Education of Blacks in the South, 1860–1935.* Chapel Hill: University of North Carolina Press, 1988.
Aptheker, Herbert. *A Documentary History of the Negro People in the United States.* New York: Citadel Press, 1951.
Baker, Henry E. *The Colored Inventor.* New York: Crisis, 1906.
Baker, Henry E. *The Colored Inventor.* New York: Arno Press, 1969.
Balch, S. W. "The Progress of Science." *Cosmopolitan* (April 1985): 762.
Balch, S. W. "Electric Motor Regulator." *Cosmopolitan* (April 1985): 761–62.
Basta, Nicholas. "Job Prospects for Minority Engineers." *Minorities Issue, Graduating Engineer* (April 1991): 78–82.
Belles, A. Gilbert. "The College Faculty, the Negro Scholar, and the Julius Rosenwald Fund." *Journal of Negro History* (October 1969): 384.
Berry, Frances B., and John W. Blassingame. *Long Memory: The Black Experience in America.* New York: Oxford University Press, 1982.

Bigglestone, W. E. "Oberlin College and Negro Students." *Journal of Negro History* (July 1971): 198.

Blau, Lauren. "Students Complain to Legislators of Recent Incidents." *Black Issues in Higher Education* (October 27, 1988): 22.

Bullock, R. W. "A Study of the Occupational Choices of Negro High School Boys." *Crisis* (September 1931): 301–03.

Burns, James M., and Jack W. Peltason. *Government by the People.* Englewood Cliffs, N.J.: Prentice-Hall, 1966.

Calloway, Thomas J. "The American Negro Artisan." *American Colored Magazine* (May 1904): 331.

Cattau, Daniel. "Forgotten Champions." *Washington Post Magazine* (June 3, 1990): 22–29.

Chase, W. M., and P. Collier. *Justice Denied: The Black Man in White America.* New York: Harcourt, Brace & World, 1970.

Christopher, M. C. "Granville T. Woods: The Plight of a Black Inventor." *Journal of Black Studies* (March 1981): 269–76.

Collison, Michelle. "College Board Aims to Boost Enrollment of Minority Students." *Chronicle of Higher Education* (June 12, 1991): A27–29.

Cox, Oliver. C. "Provisions for Graduate Education Among Negroes." *Journal of Negro Education* (January 1940): 23–28.

Daniel, Walter G. "Current Trends and Events of National Importance In Negro Education." *Journal of Negro Education* (October 1937): 662.

Davis, John W. "Negro Land Grant Colleges." *Journal of Negro Education* (July 1933): 312–28.

Downing, L. K. "The Negro in the Professions of Engineering and Architecture." *Journal of Negro Education* (June 1935): 67.

Du Bois, W.E.B. "Opinion." *Crisis* (August 1922): 151–55

Du Bois, W.E.B. "Opinion." *Crisis* (May 1926): 7.

Du Bois, W.E.B. *Dusk of Dawn.* 1st ed. New York: Harcourt, Brace & World, 1940.

Du Bois, W.E.B. *The Seventh Son.* Vol. 1. New York: Vintage Books, 1971.

Enck, H. S. "Black Self Help in the Progressive Era: The 'Northern Campaigns' of Smaller Southern Black Industrial Schools, 1900–1915." *Journal of Negro History* (January 1976): 79.

"Engineering Programs at HBCUs Working Just as Hard for Students." *Black Issues in Higher Education* (October 27, 1988).

Fallows, James. *More Like Us*. Boston: Houghton Mifflin, 1989.

Farrell, Charles S. "Successful Engineering Schools Recruit Students as Early as Junior High School." *Black Issues in Higher Education* (October 27, 1988): 23.

Ferguson, A., Jr. "Intelligence of Negroes at Camp Lee, Va." *School and Society* (June 14, 1919): 721–26.

Ferguson, A., Jr. "Intelligence of Negroes as Compared with Whites." *Current Opinion* (November 1921): 640–41.

Franklin, John H. *From Slavery to Freedom: A History of Negro Americans*. 5th ed. New York: Alfred A. Knopf, 1980.

Franklin, J. H., and A. Meier. *Black Leaders of the Twentieth Century*. Urbana: University of Illinois, 1982.

Gallison, M. "The Horizon." *Crisis* (October 1921): 83.

Gibbs, W. T. "Engineering Education In Land Grant Colleges." *Journal of Negro Education* (Fall 1952): 546.

Goldfield, David R. *Black, White and Southern: Race Relations and Southern Culture 1940 to the Present*. Baton Rouge: Louisiana State University Press, 1990.

Grimke, Archibald. "Modern Industrialism and The Negro of the United States." *American Negro Academy Occasional Papers* 16.

Hampton Institute. 1920–1950 College Catalogues.

Harris, Middleton. *The Black Book*. New York: Random House, 1974.

Harris, Nelson H. "Negro Higher Institutions of Learning in North Carolina." *Journal of Negro Education* (Summer 1962): 285–92.

Hoover, Dwight W. *Understanding Negro History*. Chicago: Quadrangle Books, 1968.

Houston, G. D. "Weaknesses in Negro Colleges." *Crisis* (July 1920): 122–25.

Howard University. 1987–1988 College Catalogues.

Hughes, L., and C. E. Meltzer. *A Picture History of Blackamericans*. New York: Crown, 1968.

Hurt, H. W. *The College Blue Book*, 4th ed. DeLand, Fla. Blue Book, 1939.

Jencks, Christopher. *Inequality: A Reassessment of the Effect of Family and Schooling in America*. New York: Basic Books, 1972.

Jencks, Christopher, and David Riesman. *The Academic Revolution*. Chicago: University of Chicago Press, 1977.

Jenkins, Martin D. "Current Trends and Events in Negro Education."
    Journal of Negro Education (January 1940): 130.
Jessup, W. A. "Standardization and Achievement." *The Educational
    Record* (April 1932): 228–38.
Johnson, Charles. *Backgrounds to Patterns of Negro Segregation.* New
    York: Thomas Y. Crowell, 1970.
Kenmitzer, Sue. "Changing America: The New Face of Science and
    Engineering." Black Issues in Higher Education (October 27,
    1988): 88.
Klein, A. E. *The Hidden Contributors: Black Scientists and Inventors in
    America.* Garden City, N.Y.: Doubleday & Co., 1971.
Kozol, Jonathan. *Death at an Early Age.* New York: Bantam Books,
    1967.
Logan, R. W., and M. R. Winston. *Dictionary of Negro Bibliography.*
    New York: W. W. Norton, 1982.
Lowitt, R., and M. Beasley, eds. *One Third of a Nation: Lorena Hickock
    Reports on the Great Depression.* Chicago: University of
    Illinois Press, 1981.
Mann, C. R. "A Study of Engineering Education." *Educational Review*
    (January 1917): 11–29.
Mays, Benjamin E. "Black Colleges, Past, Present, & Future." *Black
    Scholar* (September 1970): 32.
McAdams, Doug. *Political Process and the Development of Black
    Insurgency: 1930–1970.* Chicago: University of Chicago Press,
    1982.
McNett, Ian. *Demographic Imperatives: Implications for Educational
    Policy.* New York: American Council on Education, 1983.
Meier, A., and E. Rudwick, eds. *From Plantation to Ghetto.* New York:
    Hill and Wang, 1966.
Morris, Milton D. *The Politics of Black America.* New York: Harper and
    Row, 1975.
Moses, Wilson J. *The Golden Age of Black Nationalism, 1850–1925.*
    New York: Oxford University Press, 1978.
Myers, Gustavus. *History of Bigotry in the United States.* New York:
    Capricorn, 1960.
NACME. *Statistical Report 1986.* New York: NACME, 1986.
NACME. *Student Guide to Engineering Schools.* New York: NACME,
    1983.

Nash, Gary, and Richard Weiss, eds. *The Great Fear: Race in the Mind of America*. New York: Holt Rinehart and Winston, 1970.

National Science Foundation. *Science Indicator 1978*. Washington, D.C.: National Science Foundation, 1979.

National Science Foundation. *Women and Minorities in Science and Engineering*. Washington, D.C.: National Science Foundation, 1982.

National Science Foundation. *Characteristics of the National Sample of Scientists and Engineers 1974*. Washington, D.C.: National Science Foundation, 1976.

Patterson, H. L. *Patterson's American Educational Directory*, Vol. 3. Chicago: American Educational Co., 1936.

Pierce, Charles W. "How Electricity is Made." *The Colored American Magazine* (May 1904): 666–73.

Ploski, H. A., and W. Marr. *The Negro Almanac*. New York: Bellweather Co., 1976.

Purcell, Theodore V., and Gerald F. Cavanaugh. *Blacks in the Industrial World*. New York: The Free Press, 1971.

Ravitch, Diane. *American Reader*. New York: HarperCollins, 1990.

Reichler, Joseph, ed. *The Baseball Encyclopedia*. New York: Macmillan, 1982.

Reuter, Edward B. *The American Race Problem*. New York: Thomas Y. Crowell, 1970.

Rozwenc, Edwin C. *The Making of American Society*. Vol. 2. Boston: Allyn and Bacon, 1973.

Rudolph, Frederick. *The American College and University: A History*. New York: Vintage Books, 1962.

Simmons, William J. *Men of Mark*. Salem, N.H.: Ayer Co., 1887.

Sloan, Irving. *Blacks in America: 1492–1970*. Dobbs Ferry, N.Y.: Oceana Publications, 1971.

Smythe, Mabel. *The Black American Reference Book*. Englewood Cliffs, N.J.: Prentice-Hall, 1976.

Stuart, Karlton. *Black History and Achievement in America*. Phoenix, Ariz.: Phoenix Books, 1982.

Thompson, Charles H. "The Problem of Negro Higher Education." *Journal of Negro Education* (July 1933): 257–71.

Thompson, Charles H. "75 Years of Negro Education." *Crisis* (July 1938): 202–205.

Toppin, E. "Walter White and the Atlanta NAACP Fight for Equal Schools." *History of Education Quarterly* (Spring 1967): 37–45.

Tucker, Frank H. *The White Conscience.* New York: Frederick Unger, 1968.

U.S. Bureau of Education. *Bulletin #7, Survey of Negro Colleges and Universities.* Washington, D.C.: Bureau of Education, 1928.

U.S. Department of Commerce. Bureau of the Census. *Statistical Abstract of the United States 1990.* Washington, D.C.: Bureau of the Census, 1990.

U.S. Department of Commerce. Bureau of the Census. *Historical Statistics of the United States, Colonial Times to 1970, Parts 1 & 2.* Washington, D.C.: Bureau of the Census, 1972.

U.S. Department of Education. *Digest of Educational Statistics 1987.* Washington, D.C.: Department of Education, 1987.

U.S. Department of Education. *Digest of Educational Statistics 1990.* Washington, D.C.: Department of Education, 1990.

Vander Zanden, James W. *American Minority Relations.* Vol. 4. New York: Alfred A. Knopf, 1983.

Veysey, L. R. *The Emergence of the American University.* Chicago: University of Chicago Press, 1965.

Walker, M. Lucius. "A Prologue." *Diamond Scope* (Fall 1985): 1–2.

Weber, Susan, ed. *USA by Numbers.* Washington, D.C.: Zero Population Growth, Inc., 1988.

Weinberg, Meyer. *A Chance to Learn.* Cambridge, England: Cambridge University Press, 1979.

Weinstein, A., and F. Gattell. *The Segregation Era, 1863–1954.* New York: Oxford University Press, 1970.

Wickenden, W. E. "Who and What Determines the Educational Policies of the Engineering Schools?" *Educational Record* (July 1932): 228–38.

Wilcox, Roger. *The Psychological Consequences of Being a Black American.* New York: John Wiley & Sons, 1971.

Wilkinson, D. Y., and R. T. Taylor. *Black Man in White America.* New York: Harcourt Brace Jovanovich, 1977.

Williams, E. C. "Howard University." *Crisis* (February 1922): 157–58.

Wilson, Robin. "Colleges Start Programs to Encourage Women Who are Interested in Engineering Careers." *Chronicle of Higher Education* (June 12, 1991): A27–29.

W.P.A. *W.P.A. Guide to Washington, D.C.* New York: Pantheon Books, 1942.

DISSERTATIONS AND THESES

Abney, Diane E. "Notes on Researching Blacks at MIT Prior to the Class of 1930." Undergraduate thesis, MIT, 1983.
Wilkinson, F. D. "The School of Engineering and Architecture of Howard University: A History: 1910–1960." Master's thesis, Howard University, 1960.

CRISIS MAGAZINE ARTICLES (1912–1942)

1. "Along the Color Line." *Crisis* (November 1912).
2. "Along the Color Line." *Crisis* (July 1913): 114–16.
3. "Men of the Month." *Crisis* (August 1913): 172.
4. "Men of the Month." *Crisis* (April 1914): 42.
5. "Colleges and Their Graduates in 1914." *Crisis* (July 1914).
6. "Our Future Leaders." *Crisis* (July 1915): 137.
7. "Our Graduates." *Crisis* (July 1916): 119–27.
8. "An Architect." *Crisis* (September 1916): 239.
9. "Men of the Month." *Crisis* (February 1917): 187.
10. "Two Supervising Architects." *Crisis* (May 1917): 31.
11. "A Young Architect." *Crisis* (June 1917): 82.
12. "The Cause of Race Riots." *Crisis* (December 1919): 56–62.
13. "Higher Training of Negroes." *Crisis* (June 1921): 106.
14. "Negro Higher Education." *Crisis* (July 1922): 107.
15. "Colored Students and Graduates of 1923." *Crisis* (July 1923): 123.
16. "A Record of the Negro at College." *Crisis* (July 1925): 167.
17. "Negro Education, 1925." *Crisis* (August 1925): 166–76.
18. "The College Negro American." *Crisis* (August 1927): 185.
19. "The Far Horizon." *Crisis* (August 1927): 201–02.
20. "The Hampton Strike." *Crisis* (December 1927): 345.
21. "Education, 1928." *Crisis* (August 1928): 259–63.
22. "Along the Color Line." *Crisis* (December 1929): 145.
23. "Discrimination in Northern Colleges" *Crisis* (August 1931): 262.
24. "The Year in Negro Education." *Crisis* (August 1931): 261–62.

25. "The Year in Negro Education." *Crisis* (August 1932): 247–50.
26. "The American Negro in College, 1932–33." *Crisis* (August 1933): 181.
27. "Along the Color Line." *Crisis* (October 1933): 231.
28. "Along the Color Line." *Crisis* (March 1934): 72.,
29. "The American Negro in College, 1934–1935." *Crisis* (August 1935): 234–40.
30. "College and School News." *Crisis* (March 1941): 67.
31. "College and School News." *Crisis* (March 1941): 380.
32. "NAACP Youth Council News." *Crisis* (March 1941): 87.
33. "Negro Architect Appointed." *Crisis* (September 1941): 298.
34. "College and School News." *Crisis* (October 1941): 308.
35. "College and School News." *Crisis* (January 1942): 3.

PERSONAL INTERVIEWS

Grady, Gordon. North Shore Community College, Lynn, Massachusetts, 25 May 1988.
Livas, Henry, and family. Virginia Beach, Virginia, 20 December 1988.

PAMPHLETS

The Real McCoy. Washington, D.C.: Smithsonian Institution, 1989.

MANUSCRIPTS AND ARCHIVAL MATERIAL

Black Newspapers, 1900–1910. Howard University, Washington, D.C.
Carter G. Woodson Collection. Harvard University, Cambridge, Massachusetts.
Carter G. Woodson Papers. Smithsonian Institution, Anacostia Museum, Washington, D.C.
Commencement Programs, 1940–1950. Trade School Collection. History Collection. Hampton University, Hampton, Virginia.
Iowa State Historical Department, Office of the State Historical Society. *Palimpsest*. May/June 1985.
Sheffield School Histories. Yale University, New Haven, Connecticut.

Index

Matzeliger, Jan, 4; inventions, 12–13
Minority Introduction to Engineering (MITE), 111, 112
Montgomery, Isaiah, 2
Morgan, Garrett A., 4; awards, 12; inventions, 10–12
Morrill Act, 77
Moses, William H., 52

National Action Council for Minorities in Engineering (NACME), 107, 108, 110
National Association for the Advancement of Colored People (NAACP), 30, 43
National Association of Minority Engineering Program Administrators (NAMEPA), 107, 108, 110
National Defense Education Act, 96
National Negro Business League, 26
National Society of Black Engineers (NSBE), 107, 108, 110
National Technical Association, 44, 45
Niagara Movement, 28
Nolan, B. J., 16
North Carolina A&T College, 77–79, 113

O'Brien, E. J., 15

Pearson, James A., 69
Pittman, Sidney, 38–39
Purvis, W. B., 17

Queenan, James Weldon, 39

Race riots, 36
Repass, Maurice A., 87
Robinson, Hillyard, 51–52

SAT controversy, 101–102
Simmons, Lawrence DeWitt, 39
Skilled trades, 51, 88
Spikes, R. D., 4
State scholarships, 47–49; Maryland, 49; origin, 47
Stebbins, F. E., 16
Steward, W. H., 40

Thorne, William Miller, Jr., 39
Tillman, Ben, 31
Tribbett, Charles A., 40
Trotter, William Monroe, 26, 27
Tuskegee Institute: engineering, 68
"Tuskegee Machine," 27

United Negro Colleges, 31

Vardaman, James K., 31

Washington, Booker T., 20; conservative philosophy, 23, 24; Hampton, 23, 24; national bureau of black information, 28; political activism, 23, 24, 25, 26, 28; political power, 24, 25, 26, 29; white philanthropy, 24, 30–31
Webb, H. C., 4, 13–14
Webster, J. C., 40

About the Author

DAVID E. WHARTON served as Director of Project Interlock, a minority engineering program in the Boston area, and has worked in industry as well as higher education. Much of his writing is the result of his frustration with those who refuse to see value in programs such as Interlock. Dr. Wharton currently resides in Florida and continues to write on educational themes.